GUIDANCE MONOGRAPH SERIES

SHELLEY C. STONE

BRUCE SHERTZER

Editors

GUIDANCE MONOGRAPH SERIES

The general purpose of Houghton Mifflin's Guidance Monograph Series is to provide high quality coverage of topics which are of abiding importance in contemporary counseling and guidance practice. In a rapidly expanding field of endeavor, change and innovation are inevitably present. A trend accompanying such growth is greater and greater specialization. Specialization results in an increased demand for materials which reflect current modifications in guidance practice while simultaneously treating the field in greater depth and detail than commonly found in textbooks and brief journal articles.

The list of eminent contributors to this series assures the reader expert treatment of the areas covered. The monographs are designed for consumers with varying familiarity to the counseling and guidance field. The editors believe that the series will be useful to experienced practitioners as well as beginning students. While these groups may use the monographs with somewhat different goals in mind, both will benefit from the treatment given to content areas.

The content areas treated have been selected because of specific criteria. Among them are timeliness, practicality, and persistency of the issues involved. Above all, the editors have attempted to select topics which are of major substantive concern to counseling and guidance personnel.

Shelley C. Stone

Bruce Shertzer

INTEREST AND PERSONALITY INVENTORIES

WILLIAM C. COTTLE

BOSTON COLLEGE

HOUGHTON MIFFLIN COMPANY · BOSTON

NEW YORK · ATLANTA · GENEVA, ILL. · DALLAS · PALO ALTO

ACKNOWLEDGMENTS

It would have been impossible to collect, organize, and write this material during the past year, the busiest of my life, without the help of three persons. One is my wife, Martha, who was critic and needler par excellence. Another is my secretary, Mary E. Donovan, and the third is my graduate assistant, Donald Feron. In different ways they have earned my sincere gratitude and are as much a part of this work as I.

WM. C. COTTLE

Chestnut Hill, Mass.
May, 1967

CONTENTS

EDITORS' INTRODUCTION   xi

1. *General Considerations*   1

2. *A Professional Frame of Reference*   19

3. *The Counselor's Approach to Vocational Interest Inventories*   30

4. *Selected Vocational Interest, Preference, and Value Inventories*   50

5. *The Counselor's Approach to Personality Inventories*   70

6. *Selected Personality Inventories*   81

BIBLIOGRAPHY   107

INDEX   113

LIST OF FIGURES

1. Special SVIB profile sheet developed at the University of Kansas Guidance Bureau.   36
2. The normal curve and varied derived scores.   54
3. Edwards' description of the EPPS variables.   65
4. T-scores of mean raw scores on the MMPI for 50 blanks answered by dice and random numbers; and for 400 adult college males at Syracuse University.   74
5. T-scores of raw scores on the MMPI for a blank answered all true and one answered all false, and T-scores of mean raw scores of 179 college males at the University of Kansas.   74
6. NCS-MMPI Profile.   83
7. Two-scale analysis of the Dominance (Do) and Sociability (Sy) scales of the California Psychological Inventory.   103

LIST OF TABLES

1. Comparative Grade Placement of Selected Standardized Tests According to Various Readability Formulas and the Application of the New Forbes Formula to Items and Instructions for these Tests.   10
2. Grade Level of Reading Difficulty as Determined by the Index of Vocabulary Difficulty.   11
3. Correlation of SVIB-M and KPR-V Scores with MMPI Scores of 400 Adult Males.   40
4. Intercorrelation of SVIB-M and KPR-V Scores and Correlations Between SVIB-M, KPR-V, and Bell Adjustment Inventory Scores for 400 Adult Males.   41
5. Reported Reliabilities for the Study of Values (1951).   68
6. Intercorrelation of MMPI Scores and Correlation of MMPI and Bell Adjustment Inventory Scores for 400 Adult Males.   77
7. Correlation Coefficients and Related Estimates for Card vs. Booklet Form of the MMPI with 100 College Students.   85
8. Description of the first eleven scales of the California Psychological Inventory.   98
9. Description of the last seven scales of the California Psychological Inventory.   99

EDITORS' INTRODUCTION

This monograph brings together a tremendous amount of information crucial to the use of interest and personality inventories. Knowledge of this information is mandatory if the user of such instruments is to employ them accurately, appropriately, and ethically.

The assessment of personality and interests, whether for purposes of diagnosis, prediction of future behavior, or research, is an area of knowledge essential to the work of the counselor. Simultaneously, it should be noted that in no other area of measurement must as many precautions be exercised as in the administration and interpretation of personality and interest tests. They are not for the amateur or for individuals not well grounded in their use and interpretation. Personality inventories, in particular, are clinical instruments, and their utility depends greatly upon the skill and experience of the user.

Dr. Cottle describes the ways in which personality and interest inventories are constructed and presents useful suggestions for their administration, scoring, and interpretation. The author's work is clear, comprehensive, and useful. He believes that effective use of these inventories is contingent upon a thorough knowledge of their strengths and limitations. The author provides a description of the historical development of interest and personality testing and integrates current studies of the two areas which permit the reader to assess events in the measurement of interests and personality as they have occurred and apply to current practices.

SHELLEY C. STONE

BRUCE SHERTZER

1

....

General Considerations

Standardized tests in general, and personality and interest inventories in particular, have been subject to considerable discussion recently. Much of this has come from uninformed or ill-informed persons rather than from specialists in evaluation and measurement. For personal, rather than professional reasons, these individuals have chosen to focus discussion on the instrument rather than the person using the instrument. This distorts the perspective within which the inventories are used.

The professional person using structured personality and interest inventories or self-report questionnaires, as they are sometimes called, recognizes that most of the error in a well-constructed instrument occurs through ignorance or misuse. Even the most carefully constructed inventory is effective only within the limitations of the person who uses it or the conditions under which it is used. Therefore, criticism of an inventory should really be an evaluation of the competence of the person using it and of *his* ethics and objectives. What he knows about the instrument and how he administers or interprets it determines how effectively it works for his clients and how valid or well-protected their answers are. The user begins to acquire this knowledge by reading the manual for the inventory, reading reports about it in the literature, and by using it under supervision of someone who can be classed as an expert in its use. To ban the use of an inventory because someone

1

might misuse it is like Hitler burning books in Germany or like disbanding a protective military force because some would-be dictator might gain control of it.

It is the purpose of this monograph to explore general, basic information about personality and interest inventories using selected instruments to indicate various ways in which these inventories have been constructed and specific points to be considered in their administration, scoring, and interpretation. No professionally competent person would use data gathered from personality and interest inventories without validating these data against other client information secured from sources such as records, interview data, or even scores from other tests and inventories. All of these data should show agreement in various ways. Until the beginning counselor has acquired this skill and can perceive areas of agreement among these varied sources of data, he is not ready to use personality and interest inventories without assistance or close supervision.

Interest inventories have been used to a considerable extent with college students or adults. Much of their use with adolescents or in schools below the college level, however, has been fraught with incidents raising questions about how much they contribute. Used knowledgeably and carefully, at any educational level they are a major source of information about motivational aspects of academic and vocational behavior. Unfortunately, much of the information about them which promotes effective use is a matter of empirical evidence gathered through extensive experience and passed on through supervisory contacts or word of mouth, rather than as a part of the literature.

The two types of structured inventories in general use are classified as interest inventories and personality inventories. Both types of instruments are somewhat misnamed because each measures only selected aspects of personality contributing to the total behavior of an individual. Most of the evidence to date, however, seems to indicate very limited overlap in the information provided by these two kinds of inventories. (Cottle, 1949; Darley and Hagenah, 1955; Holland, 1966.) At the same time the lines of demarcation between them as represented by some of the more recent instruments are becoming increasingly fuzzy.

Because much of the work with interest inventories has been carried on with the two forms of the *Strong Vocational Interest Blank*, that for men (SVIB-M) and that for women (SVIB-W), and with various forms of the *Kuder Preference Record-Vocational* (KPR-V), the literature has been replete with statements that vocational interests crystallize toward the end of adolescence and only limited exploration or experimentation with new instruments designed for use below this level has occurred. This situation may be the same sort of acceptance of the status quo that produced little work on interest measurement of occupational groups below the professional level until Clark developed and published the *Minnesota Vocational Interest Inventory* (MVII).

Considered in the behavioral perspective that vocational interests lend the motivational aspect of *why* to the cognitive aspect of *what* and the affective condition of *how,* it is imperative that the beginning counselor understand what interest inventories can contribute to a client's efforts to understand and to modify behavior. It has taken a long time and much heartbreak to realize that knowledge of ability is simply not enough. An individual not only must be *able* to do something and be in an emotional state that permits him to do it, but he must also *want* to do it before he achieves success in this effort.

Although interest inventories have been developing for half a century, it is only now that their real worth is being realized. Used carefully and in conjunction with all other client data, they, along with inventories of goals, attitudes, and values, become the *why* of behavior. Interest inventories will be stressed here rather than inventories of goals, attitudes, and values because more research has been done with the former than with the latter.

Structured personality inventories have had a slower and somewhat more controversial growth. Starting with instruments like the *Woodworth Psychoneurotic Inventory* of World War I and followed by the various forms of the *Bell Adjustment Inventories,* the *Humm-Wadsworth Inventory* and the *Bernreuter Personality Inventory,* learning to use personality inventories became an art and beclouded the scientific approach to data collection and synthesis now emerging with the computerized approach to interpreting the *Minnesota Multiphasic Personality Inventory* (MMPI) (Kleinmuntz, 1963). Too much time and effort was focused on identifying the abnormal person rather than on describing his more numerous normal brothers. It has taken a long time to realize that these inventories simply describe the affective conditions or *how* a person behaves, not *why.* In this sense, however, they are an essential part of the total picture of his behavior. Considered in this setting, and putting aside for the moment the involved question of norms and abnormality, these inventories, when used effectively, can make an important contribution to counseling. To do this, they must be considered as furnishing information about how a person sees himself interacting with others. Regardless of the reality of the situation as perceived by society, these inventories tell how his behavior appears to the respondent and thus tell him and his counselor how best to utilize such knowledge to modify behavior for more effective life choices. Whether Horney's description of "moving toward or away from people" as an aspect of describing behavior is used, or whether scores from these inventories are considered usual aspects of social behavior, or as a major phase of describing client self-concept, they are important and have much to contribute to counseling in the hands of those who know how to use them.

Construction

One problem in the use of personality and interest inventories is the time it takes a beginning counselor to realize that their construction in part determines the kind of information they provide and also dictates how the information should be used. This construction has evolved around the trait-factor approach to describing behavior and has been confused further by the use of criterion groups to provide evidence of the validity of selected instruments. In addition, the use of normative groups, rather than an ipsative, individual, or idiosyncratic approach in interpretation of their meaning, has complicated the discussion with a client of the meaning of his scores from these inventories.

In the construction of both personality and interest inventories, the first approach was an empirical one. Data which had evidenced possibilities of differentiating among individuals or among groups of individuals were made into forced-choice items of varied types on the basis of content validity; that is, items which dealt with home conditions, as in the *Bell Adjustment Inventories,* were grouped and scored to produce a "Home Adjustment Scale." In like manner other scales were constructed to measure "Health Adjustment," "Social Adjustment," or "Emotional Adjustment." In the KPR-V, these became triads of items with the subject required to indicate most and least areas of interest. In the early forms of the SVIB one indicated "Like," "Indifferent," or "Dislike" to 400 items. In the MMPI, the choices were "True," "False," or "Cannot Say." For the *Guilford-Zimmerman Temperament Survey* (GZTS) or the *California Psychological Inventory* (CPI), they were "Yes," "No," or left blank. Regardless of how the choices were limited, limitation was necessary if an objective, relatively simple scoring system was to be possible. Scoring ease and objectivity, in the case of the SVIB, were complicated by the necessity of weighting items for maximum discrimination. Thus, such a simple issue as the method of scoring items created complications in use and in interpretation of the inventory. The discovery of response-set tendencies connected with these answers further complicated interpretation and raised pertinent questions about the meaning of the scores. All of these elements add to the confusion of the beginning counselor trying to learn how to use the inventory.

The way in which the inventory was developed also determines in part the way it can be used and interpreted. Kuder used a large pool of items and by item analysis (internal consistency) methods produced scales composed of items which had a high correlation with each other and as low a correlation as possible with items in other scales of the inventory. These relatively independent scales were then inspected for content, and names appropriate to this content, such as "Mechanical," "Computational," or "Literary," were chosen for each scale. Focusing on item analysis techniques is one way to produce an inventory.

Another approach is that illustrated by the *Minnesota Personality Scale* (Darley and McNamara, 1943) or the GZTS. These inventories are a product of factor analysis techniques. Factor analysis is a statistical process designed to achieve one of three purposes. It can be used to isolate common factors in a body of data, it can be used to identify a general factor and specific factors pervading a set of data, or it can be used to predict performance from scores on a series of variables. Ordinarily the use of factor analysis to construct interest and personality inventories has as its major purpose the isolation of common factors occurring in the data. Then names are given to these factors in much the same fashion as Kuder named his scales; that is, the variables contributing the most weight to each factor are inspected and their nature is inferred by the name of the new factor, such as, "Economic Conservatism," in the case of the *Minnesota Personality Scale* (MPS) or "General Activity vs. Inactivity," or "Ascendance vs. Submissiveness," in the case of the GZTS. This process is somewhat more complex for personality and interest inventories than for tests of intelligence and achievement. The latter evidence only positive correlations and have meaning in only one direction, such as "Verbal" or "Numerical." Personality and interest inventories, however, evidence positive *and* negative relationships. Thus meaning in two directions or a bipolar interpretation must be educed, as indicated by the GZTS scale, "Sociability vs. Shyness," or the factor "Science vs. Business" found in factorial studies of the SVIB and the KPR-V (Cottle, 1949).

A third approach to the construction of personality and interest inventories involves a combination of item analysis techniques and the use of criterion groups. Here, as in the construction of the SVIB or the MMPI, a group representing a given complex or syndrome of behavior is selected for comparison with some other group representing a contrasting point of reference. In the case of the occupational groups on the SVIB, the criterion groups would be "Physicians," "Lawyers," or "Engineers" whose answers to the 400 items of the inventory are compared to those of all the other "professional and managerial" groups combined into a general "point of reference" group. Items showing the greatest differences are then weighted and scored as the "Physician Key," the "Lawyer Key," or the "Engineer Key." Thus, by construction, they show responses of a given criterion group and demonstrate the validity of these scales to identify persons with interests like physicians, lawyers or engineers who responded to the SVIB. Kreidt (1949) and Strong and Tucker (1952) have also demonstrated that it is possible to use this technique to make even finer distinctions. Kreidt used a "Psychologist-in-general" group as a point of reference to distinguish or differentiate differences in interest among clinical, guidance, industrial, and experimental psychologists. In like manner, Strong and Tucker used "physicians-in-general" to distinguish among the interests of internal medicine specialists, psychiatrists, pathologists, and surgeons.

In the case of the MMPI, the criterion groups used by Hathaway and McKinley (1943) were a series of psychiatrically diagnosed clinical groups compared with a people-in-general group not under treatment in order to identify items related to a given abnormal syndrome. For example, responses of a group of manic-depressives in the depressive phase were used as the basis for the "Depression" scale of the MMPI. This method and an internal consistency method similar to that used by Kuder are the two processes used to create the original nine clinical scales of the MMPI. The many new scales of the MMPI described in Dahlstrom and Welsh (1960) are constructed using this method of criterion groups defined as representing a given syndrome of behavior. Gough (1956) used a refinement of the criterion group process together with an adjective checklist to create and validate the eighteen scales of the *California Psychological Inventory*. Cottle (1966) has also used this process in the educational setting to develop male and female dropout scales, a male delinquency scale, a non-achiever scale and a linguistic-nonlinguistic scale for the *School Interest Inventory* (SII).

Still a fourth approach to the development of the modern inventory is that used in the *Edwards Personal Preference Schedule* (EPPS). In creating this inventory, Edwards was impressed with the tendency of individuals to produce the response they felt would be most "socially acceptable" in a given situation. This tendency has been called "social desirability" response set. Edwards attempted to control for this tendency by identifying levels or degrees of social desirability response set connected with the various items he proposed to use in his inventory. He then matched in each item a pair of responses of approximately equal "social desirability." By this means, a person choosing one of the two responses, theoretically at least, was not motivated by the tendency to choose one response as the more socially desirable and this type of response set would not bias his answer. Research to date indicates that Edwards was only moderately successful in controlling for "social desirability" response set. By asking respondents to choose from matched pairs, however, he was able to eliminate another response set usually referred to as "acquiescence." "Acquiescence" response set involves the tendency to answer "yes" or "true" more frequently than "no" or "false" or vice versa. This problem of response sets creates some interesting questions about their effect on test interpretation and will be discussed in some detail later.

Actually, if one includes the early process of using items of demonstrated content validity to construct personality and interest inventories, the material above has described five different methods of developing inventories which sample affective and motivational aspects of behavior. Inventories created by these processes and the interaction of their evidence with each other are a part of the attempt to interpret behavior in terms of those data.

Administration

The major points to be considered in the administration of any personality and interest inventory are:

1. Administration, scoring, and interpretation should be handled by professionally trained and competent persons.

2. Most persons taking such an inventory do so voluntarily as a part of counseling or psychotherapy. Where an inventory is required as a part of educational or occupational selection, its chief purpose is to screen out individuals who are apt to experience failure or who are not congruent with the aims of the organization. These persons should have the right to refuse to take the inventory if they wish to or to take it through an independent agency.

3. Inventories are administered according to a standardized set of instructions and taken by persons with a serious purpose. These persons should be instructed to respond as rapidly as possible even though there is no time limit. In general, a first response tends to be more descriptive of the respondent than changed or pondered responses. Thus, hurrying through the items tends to produce a more typical description of these aspects of the respondent's behavior.

4. Answer sheets are machine-scored under most circumstances and have little or no meaning until scores on the various scales are reported in profile form. Inspecting answers to any given item is seldom done, except to ascertain that the answer sheet has been completed properly.

5. If answer sheets are sent away to be scored, the scoring service should be asked to return them with the reported scores or profiles. Otherwise, checking for errors is not possible. Some scoring services

do not return answer sheets unless requested to do so. Someone in the school should know how to hand-score the inventory to check on mistakes in scoring, the most common source of error.

6. Responses to a single item of a given scale have little or no meaning by themselves. It is the cumulative effect of responses to a scale which indicates a tendency toward a given kind of behavior.

7. Because of the changing nature of behavior measured by personality and interest inventories, it is questionable how useful scores from inventories taken more than three months previous will prove to be. They may be useful for research purposes, but a current test will usually be much more valid for counseling purposes.

8. The private nature of the inventory data precludes any detailed discussion of it with anyone but the client or professional colleagues who will use the data professionally.

9. Any unusual behavior of the client during the time he is completing the inventory should be recorded and made a part of the profile report of scores.

10. Profiles or scores should be considered to be held in trust for the individual or for the organization. They should be released only to professionally competent persons with a legitimate right to request them.

11. It is assumed that the normative group for each inventory is an appropriate one against which to compare the person to whom the inventory is given.

12. It is assumed that the reading level of the inventory fits the person to whom it is administered.

Forbes and Cottle (1953) carried out a study to determine objectively the reading difficulty of standardized tests commonly used in counseling and to develop a new and simplified method for determining the reading level of these tests.

Five of the more popular techniques for evaluating the reading difficulty of printed matter were critically analyzed in relation to the same group of standardized tests. The Dale-Chall, Flesch, Lorge, Lewerenz, and Yoakam formulas were applied to 27 tests commonly used for counseling at various educational levels. The mean score of reading difficulty was then obtained for each test. The choice of the tests to be used in this study was determined from previous studies made upon test preference.

The five formulas selected for study are techniques for measuring readability. They present several factors which have been used for determining reading difficulty of printed matter, such as word difficulty, prepositional phrases, sentence length, number of syllables per hundred words, number of different words, and percentages of words beginning with certain letters. Each of the formulas has been carefully developed and exhibits considerable reliability and validity. In the Yoakam formula, "hard words" vary in difficulty according to their frequency and range of occurrence beyond the most common four thousand words. The Lewerenz formula relies solely on word difficulty, basing vocabulary difficulty on words with certain initial letters. The Flesch formula considers the length of the word as the index of difficulty and the more syllables a word has the more difficult it is. The Dale-Chall formula uses a list of three thousand words and any word not appearing on this list is considered difficult. The Lorge formula considers a "hard word" to be any word other than the 769 words that are common to the first one thousand most frequent English words on the Thorndike list and the first thousand words known most frequently by children entering first grade.

The grade level scores obtained for each test from the five formulas were averaged to obtain a mean grade level reading difficulty score for each test. These mean scores were taken as criterion grade level scores of reading difficulty for these selected tests. They are shown in Table 1.

The scores obtained from the Forbes-Cottle article for the reading level of each test correlated slightly over .95 with the mean of the five formulas and ranged between .95 and .72 for the five formulas.

The knowledge of grammar needed to apply the five formulas is considerable. Also, the amount of time required by these methods makes them quite laborious. More than ten hours are required to apply some formulas to a single test. The average amount of time for the working of a single formula on a single test is more than two and one-half hours. The simplified Forbes method requires approximately one-half hour per test.

Word difficulty was used as a common factor in all five formulas studied. It is also evident from a review of the literature that word difficulty is basic to the readability of all printed matter.

The exact method of applying the new formula is listed as follows (Forbes and Cottle, 1953):

1. Three samples of 100 words each were taken from the tests to be analyzed. The samples were selected in each test at the beginning, middle and end. The only requirements for the samples were that they consist of an even hundred words, that each sample begin with the first word of an item, and the vocabulary tests be omitted from the samples. It seemed only fair to omit the vocabulary sections in order to get the average reading difficulty of the standardized tests.

It seemed easiest to begin with the first word of the item of a test and count the first hundred word sample exactly. The middle sample was selected as near the midpoint of the test as possible. Starting with

TABLE 1

Comparative Grade Placement of Selected Standardized Tests According to Various Readability Formulas and the Application of the New Forbes Formula to Items and Instructions for these Tests

Test	Dale-Chall	Flesch	Lorge	Lewer-enz	Yoakam	Av. of Five Formulas	Forbes Items	Forbes Instructions
MMPI	5.5	6.1	4.4	6.2	4.8	5.4	6.5	7.3
School Inventory	5.6	6.3	5.0	7.6	3.3	5.5	5.0	7.2
Calif. Test Pers.	6.2	7.2	5.3	5.7	6.6	6.2	7.1	6.3
AGCT	5.9	11.0	5.7	8.0	4.0	6.9	6.2	6.1
Guilford-Zimmerman	6.0	7.5	5.6	8.2	7.3	6.9	7.4	8.3
Otis Q-S	6.1	7.1	5.8	8.2	7.7	7.0	7.6	6.4
Adjustment Inv.	6.4	9.1	6.1	7.7	8.0	7.7	7.8	6.1
Minn. Pers. Scale	6.5	9.1	6.2	6.5	10.8	7.8	8.8	8.2
Mooney	6.1	8.3	6.0	8.7	11.0	8.1	8.9	7.2
Bernreuter	6.7	8.4	6.7	7.3	11.9	8.2	9.1	7.0
CTMM	7.2	10.8	8.8	8.0	6.7	8.3	9.1	6.3
Stanford Ach.	7.0	8.4	7.0	6.4	14.5	8.7	10.6	6.7
Kuder CM	7.3	8.5	7.7	7.8	12.5	8.7	9.7	8.3
Otis Employ.	6.3	7.9	6.3	9.3	14.3	8.8	9.1	6.4
Henmon-Nelson	6.6	9.2	6.1	11.3	12.6	9.1	9.8	5.0
Iowa Silent	8.0	11.4	7.9	9.1	10.1	9.3	9.3	6.7
Lee-Thorpe	8.0	10.0	7.9	7.8	13.6	9.5	10.3	7.6
Kuder BB	7.6	9.2	7.6	8.5	14.5	9.5	10.7	7.9
SRA Reading	8.3	13.2	8.5	9.9	12.6	10.5	9.8	6.8
Cleeton	8.4	14.4	7.4	8.3	16.0*	10.9	12.5	6.9
Strong Voc. Int.	8.9	15.8	6.7	12.0	13.3	11.4	10.2	8.5
Coop. Reading	8.7	14.0	9.9	10.4	14.0	11.4	10.4	7.8
Minn. Reading	9.0	13.2	9.4	9.7	16.0*	11.5	11.9	9.2
Ohio State Psy.	10.7	16.5*	9.6	9.0	11.8	11.5	11.5	7.3
ACE	8.5	16.1	8.5	9.4	16.0*	11.7	12.7	7.6
Coop. Gen. Cult.	8.5	15.6	10.7	10.3	16.0*	12.2	Coll.	7.5
Study of Values	9.1	16.1	9.6	12.7	16.0*	12.7	12.4	9.6

* Estimate of the grade; the formulas did not indicate grades at these levels.
Reprinted with permission from Forbes, F. W., and W. C. Cottle, "A New Method for Determining Readability of Standardized Tests." *Journal of Applied Psychology,* Vol. 37, 1953, p. 186.

the middle item count backward to the initial word of an item close to fifty words back. The remainder of the middle one hundred word sample was secured by counting the difference from one hundred in words beyond this middle item. The third sample was taken by counting backwards from the last word of the test items until one hundred words were counted. Should the one hundred words end within an item, proceed counting backwards until the first word of an item is reached, then in order to get exactly one hundred words omit the number over one hundred at the end of the sample.

2. Each word that appeared difficult to the grader was written on a sheet of paper. These words were then found in the 1942 *Thorndike*

TABLE 2

Grade Level of Reading Difficulty as Determined by the Index of Vocabulary Difficulty

Index of Vocabulary Difficulty	Grade Level
1.4510 and above	College
1.2510 to 1.4509	12th grade
1.0510 to 1.2509	11th grade
.8510 to 1.0509	10th grade
.6510 to .8509	9th grade
.4510 to .6509	8th grade
.2510 to .4509	7th grade
.0510 to .2509	6th grade
.0509 and below	5th grade

Reprinted with permission from Forbes, F. W., and W. C. Cottle, "A New Method for Determining Readability of Standardized Tests." *Journal of Applied Psychology*, Vol. 37, 1953, p. 188.

Junior Century Dictionary. The number following the definition in this dictionary is the weight for that word. These numbers range from one to twenty representing the first twenty successive thousands of words most commonly used in the English language. Only words above the most frequently used four thousand words were given a weight. Any word having a weight of four or above was considered a difficult word and its weight was listed. Words used more than once in the samples were given their weights each time they were used.

3. The weights for the three samples were totaled and divided by the number of words in the samples, 300 in this case. This gave *index of vocabulary difficulty* for the standardized tests.

4. Using the indices of vocabulary difficulty obtained from the above three steps, refer to Table 2 in order to determine grade level of difficulty of the printed matter in the test being analyzed. Grade level scores may be interpolated to the nearest tenth of a grade.

5. The reading difficulty was also figured for the instructions for each of the tests analyzed. The samples in some cases included all directions to the tests when they consisted of 300 words or less; other samplings followed the procedure outlined above for the test, that is, taking 100 word samples at three points throughout the instructions.

There is little room for decisions to be made by the scorer who uses the Forbes method since the words are weighted in accordance with an accepted word list. If a variant of a word or a hyphenated word does not appear in this list, no weight is given. Only words that appear in the *Thorndike Junior Century Dictionary* (1942) are given weights.

Scoring

Whether scoring is handled on a local or a national basis depends on the inventory and upon the resources available to the agency. Some inventories, like the SVIB, are too complex or expensive to hand-score and are best handled by sending them to centers especially equipped to score them. Including mailing costs, scoring at national centers is usually less expensive and more accurate than the cost of hand-scoring locally or rental of machines for local scoring. Local scoring also requires the training of personnel who, if they are competent in the job, are bright enough so that they use it only as a stepping stone to some other employment. The constant training of replacement personnel is an expense often overlooked in computing local versus national costs of scoring. Machine-scoring, local or national, produces a lower percent of error, and the more highly organized and trained personnel in a national scoring center tend to make fewer errors. Some inventories use a special answer sheet which is only set up for use on a special scoring machine and cannot be scored on local equipment.

For these reasons, most of the large test publishing firms quote a price for national scoring which they arrange with organizations equipped to do scoring of inventories on a mass basis. Such organizations as Measurement Research Center in Iowa City and Testscor or National Computer Systems in Minneapolis are usually able to score personality and interest inventories less expensively than local scoring when all actual costs are compared. These sources should be explored before local scoring is considered. Use of professionals, such as teachers or counselors, to do hand-scoring is a waste of expensive, highly skilled workers to do labor a machine can handle cheaper. It is like hiring counselors and then having them call the homes of all students absent from school to ask why they are absent. This is a task anyone who can use a telephone can perform and is a waste of expensive or limited counseling time. Even though some inventories like the KPR-V or the GZTS are easy to hand-score, it is usually less expensive in the long run to have them scored at a national scoring service.

At the same time, there is an advantage to having someone available in the local area who knows how to hand-score tests. When a counselor and a client decide that scores from a personality or interest inventory do not agree with the rest of the client data which have been synthesized, the first logical step is to check the scoring of the inventory. Often an error in scoring causes the discrepancy. Unless a quick method of checking by hand-scoring the questionable material is available, the data may just have to be omitted or disregarded if there is not time to return it to the national scoring center. Whether it is checked locally or nationally, the original answer sheet is required. This is why an earlier statement suggested that a request to return all answer sheets accompany tests sent away to be scored. Another reason is that it may become necessary to score extra scales not scored originally as a result of reviewing the total synthesis of client data or because of an unforeseen change in client objectives. Thus, someone on the local scene who knows how to hand-score the inventories can save considerable time for the client or a busy counselor. This might be the supervisor or even someone outside the agency but readily available. However, there should be someone *in* the agency sufficiently familiar with scoring procedures to serve as a consultant on questionable scores.

It can be seen from this discussion that the scoring procedure in part contributes to the amount of error involved in the scores and therefore affects the reliability and validity of the inventory. Other factors contributing to the reliability of the scales of the inventory would be the relatively fixed versus the changeable nature of the behavior being measured, the method by which reliability is computed, the heterogeneity versus homogeneity of items, or the number of items included in the scale and the circumstances in which the inventory was administered.

A major problem in estimating the reliability of any scale on an inventory, that is, the amount of error involved in using the score with an individual or a group, is the fact that affective and motivational aspects of behavior are more subject to change than are cognitive or intellectual aspects of behavior. As an individual matures, his vocational interests may intensify or changing environmental or personal attributes may cause these measured interests to change also. Ordinarily, drastic changes are produced only by drastic differences in self or environmental perceptions. However, varied developmental differences in individuals are pronounced enough to produce lowered reliabilities when behavior for a group of persons is being evaluated over a period of time. Personality inventories also tend to show similar lowered reliabilities. Attention should be given to the kind of behavior being measured by a given scale of a personality inventory. If it purports to measure *depression,* the elements contributing to this behavioral syndrome may vary enough over a period of time to produce a lowered reliability coefficient in contrast to the less changing behavior involved in a dominance-submission scale. This in part is also reflected in the method of computing reliability. When two administrations of the inventory are compared in computing reliability, the changing nature of the behavior has more effect. When a single administration of the inventory is used to compute reliability, the changing nature of the behavior has less effect. For most personality and interest inventories, a single administration of the inventory should be used to compute reliabilities. While the split-half method of computing reliability can be used if the items are quite similar, the fact that many scales contain dissimilar items usually indicates that it is more proper to use the Kuder-Richardson Formula 20 in figuring reliability. This formula is based upon the cumulation of difficulties of each item in the scale and thus conveys the contribution of each item to the reliability of the scale.

In addition to the heterogeneous nature of the items in a given scale, the actual number of items may affect the reliabilities of the scale. In general, the greater the number of items (within the limits of feasibility), the higher the reliabilities tend to be.

Another series of conditions which limit the obtained reliabilities centers around the nature of the subjects used and the physical conditions of the testing situation. For example, it is possible that, when abnormal subjects are tested, particularly if there is a considerable time lapse between testings in a test-retest situation, the reliabilities will be lower because of inconsistencies or actual changes in behavior. At least there is evidence (Hathaway and McKinley, 1943) that reliabilities secured on mental patients in general tend to be lower than those secured on persons not under treatment (college students). In like manner, college students may differ somewhat from a general adult population, particularly when tested right before a holiday or semester exams. The counselor should be sure that he uses reliabilities secured on a normative group similar to the client with whom he is using the inventory.

The physical condition or comfort of the subjects at the time of testing, even if they are of approximately the same general category as the client, may distort the reliabilities of the inventory. In a small group, individuals who are ill or about to be ill, can reduce reliabilities. The discomfort of a hot room, inadequate ventilation, the use of lap boards, poor lighting, or crowding may contribute to lowered reliabilities.

All of these factors producing lowered reliabilities may in turn have an effect on the validity of scales of personality and interest inventories. Unless behavior is stable, consistent, and approximately equivalent from one time to another, it is difficult to distinguish how valid the estimates represented by scores on these inventories will be in discussing current behavior and in predicting future behavior.

Validity here has to be considered in light of counselor and client purpose. For the counselor, the worth of the scores lies in helping him understand or cross-validate what a client tells him, and in using these data to help the client arrive at predictions or probabilities of future behavior based on the data as client and counselor perceive them. To the client, the worth is based on two separate elements. One is his perception of himself in his responses to items which produced the scores. The other is his ability to accept and use the results of testing to modify behavior in future life choices. In the first instance, the client may not be able to respond candidly to the items of the inventory. He may not be able to face himself as he really is *or* he may not wish others, including the counselor, to perceive him the way he perceives himself. Thus he distorts his responses, usually without being aware that he is doing so, and the scores are less valid in describing him. One often encounters the question about forced choice items, "What does *frequent* mean in the item, 'Do you have *frequent* colds?'" or "What would have happened if the client had not had to choose *most* and *least liked* among three items, all of which he disliked?" Actually it is the cumulative impact of a group of items rather than the effect of one item which conveys the information secured from these inventories. In the case of the first item listed above, it is the effect created by a series of responses to items about a client's physical condition that indicates he is, or is not, more concerned about his health than most people in the normative group for the scale. In like manner, it is the accumulation of responses to activities liked most or liked least that determines high and low or most and least acceptable areas of vocational interest. In this sense, then, the counselor needs other data as a cross-validation of how the client has responded to the inventory. He can get this from internal sources of validation, such as patterns of occupational and non-occupational scores on the SVIB. For example, if the occupational scores in Group V, Social Welfare Scales, are high, the Interest Maturity Scale should be high and usually the Masculinity-Femininity Scale shows a femininity score. Or, he can get it from actual validation scales built into the inventory, like the "communality" scale of the CPI, or the four validating scales of the MMPI. He must also cross-check inventory scores with client data secured from non-test sources, such as records or interview data. But whatever the source, the more he knows about synthesizing client data, the more validly he contributes to client knowledge and the more effective client decisions can be. This leads directly into the interpretations of the scores that the counselor gives the client.

Interpretation

It should be noted first that the client knows nothing about how to interpret test scores or profiles. For this reason, the counselor must decide what he should tell the client about the scores and how he should discuss this. If the information is to be useful, the client must be able to accept and use it to change behavior or make decisions about future choices. He can do this only if the language choices of the counselor and the meaning of the scores are presented in a fashion that minimizes the amount of threat that is involved. Whether the counselor shows the profile to the client or only discusses its meaning does not seem to matter very much.

One purpose of the counselor is to show scores that are enough different from the average part of the normative group to show how the client differs from them. For most inventories, this means scores *below* the 16th percentile or a *T*-score of 40 and *above* the 84th percentile or a *T*-score of 60. One exception to this is the KPR-V where the 25th and the 75th percentiles are used. A simple expedient is to draw a line across the profile or an arrow at these points and say to the client, "Unless your scores are above and below these lines or arrows, your answers do not describe you as being different from most of the people on whom the inventory was standardized." It is optional whether the client's scores in the average group are discussed. The important point is to use the term "average group" or "average scores" and *not* "normal group." Most clients are apt to infer that, if their score is not in the "normal group," they are abnormal. It is better therefore, to avoid use of the word *"normal"* in discussing personality and interest inventory scores.

It is also wise to experiment with terms with which the counselor feels comfortable and which are simple and clear enough that most clients understand them. This usually means avoidance of technical and professional terms, i.e., scores should be discussed in *client* words. When the counselor uses the same words over and over with different clients to convey the meaning of scores, he is apt to feel that his interpretations are becoming boring. He needs to remember that he is the only one who hears the same description repeatedly. When he finds a useful way of describing a score to clients, he should use it. This method also has the advantage of helping the counselor remember what he has said to the client when he makes notes of his interview.

Whether the counselor discusses these scores in the second person or uses a phrase like "People with scores like these tend to . . ." depends on his style and what he feels the client can accept best. This means the counselor has to have spent time in self-evaluation through analyzing interview tapes and similar processes to find the methods most suitable to him and with which he feels most comfortable. It also means he has to know enough about a given client that he can judge what that client will be comfortable discussing. It is advisable to pause after pointing out the meaning of a given score to see whether the client wants to discuss it in detail. Even though the counselor is always watching the client during the process of interpreting scores, facial expression, gestures, or bodily posture of the client may not give the counselor enough information and he may even want to ask, "Is that clear to you?" Use of simple, clear, common terminology decreases the need to do this.

The effect of words the counselor chooses can have considerable impact on client behavior and acceptance of inventory data. When working with an inventory like the GZTS, this is important. The terms that are used to describe these ten bipolar traits on the profile are often unacceptable to clients. Many persons do not like to be told they are "shy" or "seclusive," even if they know they are. They are usually able to accept the statement that "they would rather be a follower than a leader." Or, in the case of masculinity-femininity scores found on most of these inventories it is more effective to tell a boy with a high femininity score that his score shows an interest in linguistic behavior based on a knowledge of and contact with people and on speaking, listening, reading, or writing activities. Conversely, it is more effective to tell a girl with a high masculinity score that this means an interest in nonlinguistic behavior based on non-word symbols and an interest in scientific or mechanical processes, inanimate objects, and physical activities. Clients seem more able to accept these specific descriptions of behavior than they do the older, vaguer terms, *masculinity* or *femininity* (Terman and Miles, 1936).

It is sometimes a moot question whether normative or ipsative scores should be used in interpretations with clients. If counselor and client feel that self-perceptions are more important, the use of ipsative scoring which shows the high and low areas, for that client only, may be more profitable. For example, rather than using the general, vague reference groups for the KPR-V, the counselor could compute the proportion of scored responses to total possible responses for each scale and thus identify highest to lowest scores on all of these scales for that given client. Or he could take the actual raw score on each of the fifteen scales of the EPPS which each have 28 possible items and arrange these from highest to lowest for a given client only.

However, if the important issue is how this client's behavior compares to other persons, the use of scores comparing him to the normative group on whom the inventory was standardized will be more practical.

These are some of the general considerations in any attempt to discuss scores from inventories with clients. More specific interpretations pertaining to a given type of inventory will be considered when the inventories are discussed later.

Succeeding Chapters

The succeeding chapters will deal with professional attitudes toward using personality and interest inventories and with examples of material important in the use of selected inventories.

Obviously, it is impossible to discuss all the inventories which could be used in the school setting. For this reason, the chapter on interest inventories will deal with the *Kuder Preference Record-Vocational* and the *Strong Vocational Interest Blanks,* because they have had the most widespread use and the most copious research is carried out with them. The *Minnesota Vocational Interest Inventory* will be discussed also as one of the newest instruments which seems to offer promise.

As far as structured personality inventories are concerned, the *Minnesota Multiphasic Personality Inventory* has had by far the most copious use in research and in varied settings. Other personality inventories have been chosen because they typify certain types of construction, such as the factor analysis techniques used to produce the *Guilford-Zimmerman Temperament Survey* or the attempt to control response set exemplified by the *Edwards Personal Preference Schedule.* The *Allport-Vernon-Lindzey Study of Values* is included as a typical attempt to quantify value aspects of behavior. The *California Psychological Inventory* will be included because of the research that has been done with it among "relatively normal" high school and college groups.

2

A Professional
Frame of Reference

A major reason for much of the difficulty surrounding the use of personality and interest inventories in the school has been the lack of a clear understanding of their purpose on the part of the profession. As a consequence, clear description of their use has not been possible to clients, to parents, or to agency or government personnel (APA, 1966b) not trained in use of these inventories. This creates a situation where people favor or oppose these inventories without really knowing why. Even professional persons doing counseling, psychotherapy, or selection have been divided in their opinions of the effectiveness of structured inventories without a factual basis for such opinions. In many cases they have failed to support professional use of such inventories or have not clearly indicated how they are to be used. This is typified by statements about personality inventories like that of Karl Menninger (1965) to a congressional committee:

> I do not know whether what they measure is personality. I would not even want to accept that description, that definition. Paper-and-pencil tests, with answers put down by the individual himself and added up to a number of scales, do not impress me as very useful. Having invented one or two myself, I recognize that.

Later in his testimony he said, "I am not competent to apply these tests, you know." It is this lack of knowledge about inventories and even a failure to become informed about them that has impeded their effective use in the professional setting.

Ellis (1953), in discussing validity of personality inventories, has also helped to becloud the issue. He says,

> . . . since personality inventories depend, in the last analysis, on printed questions, and since virtually no one claims for them the advantage of getting unconscious and semiconscious material which effective clinical use of interview and projective methods are generally conceded to some extent to uncover, it is difficult to see why clinicians should spend considerable time first mastering and then using these inventories. The clinical psychologist who cannot in the time it now takes a trained worker to administer, score and interpret a test like the MMPI according to the best recommendations of its authors, get much more pertinent, incisive, and depth-centered 'personality' material from a straightforward interview technique would hardly appear to be worth his salt.

Anyone who uses personality inventories like the *Minnesota Multiphasic Personality Inventory* should be professionally capable of eliciting by the use of interview processes the same data that the MMPI produces. The major purpose in using the MMPI instead is to permit clerks or psychological technicians under the supervision of a more highly trained person to provide this information, thus saving time for the more highly trained counselor or counseling psychologist to perform more specialized functions. This is especially important in a period of extreme shortages of trained professional personnel.

To produce the same information the *Strong Vocational Interest Blanks* (SVIB) or the *Minnesota Vocational Interest Inventory* (MVII) provide would take extensive interviews, and still the comparison with occupational groups would be tenuous or absent. These instruments provide information the counselor can elicit in no other way because they show how a client's vocational interests resemble, or fail to resemble, the inventoried interests of various occupational groups. It is true that no one knows what the measured interests of these criterion groups might have been during adolescence, but empirical evidence from counseling indicates that adolescents with scores like engineers or business detail workers go on to enter these professions and some of Strong's work (1955) indicates high or low areas of interests remain quite stable from college on through adult life.

In general, one might say that when these inventories are used as they were intended to be used or as research has indicated they can be used, they provide an effective help to the counselor and his client. To use them effectively, the counselor needs to know how they were intended to be used and what added use research points out. The counselor needs to identify the professional experts and to know what they can tell him about these inventories.

The inventories themselves are an attempt to quantify and make objective the feeling reactions of the person who takes them. In the case of the interest inventories, they attempt to provide a score indicating feelings of pleasantness-unpleasantness or like-dislike to varied environmental stimuli (Fryer, 1931). This permits a comparison with various normative groups, such as the comparison of client interests with the interests of males or females in various sorts of activities Kuder Preference Record-Vocational (KPR-V) or with those of males or females in various occupational groups (SVIB or MVII). When personality inventories are used, they present a score reflecting feelings about self or non-self (feelings about others or objects outside the respondent to which he is reacting).

Whichever kind of inventory is used, it reflects the individual's reaction to an occurrence in the present or something which has happened in the past. It is an expression of *what* a person feels, not *why* he feels this way. In this sense, the scores from the inventory serve as indicators of the direction further investigation must take in order to achieve a clearer statement of probabilities in helping a client predict future behavior. They may also indicate the processes or instruments to use in order to clarify further the client decisions about future choices.

The most effective approach to the use of such scores is to consider them as global indicators of respondent behavior. There are some persons who are willing to sit down with a client and go over the client response to each item. This is a waste of time, unless the purpose is to find out whether an error has occurred. When a client questions whether such scores really describe him, a check may be necessary to see whether he answered items in a way that achieves this or whether the items were scored properly. Just to go through the items one by one for other purposes is relatively useless because it is the *cumulative impact* of a series of items on a given scale which provides a meaningful score. In the same sense, part scores on an inventory may be equally useless or misleading. There may not be enough items involved in producing the part score to provide sufficient reliability to warrant the use of such a score, or the part score by itself may not give enough information about its interaction with other parts of the inventory to warrant using or interpreting it alone. Interpretation in terms of *patterns* of scores provides a clearer picture of respondent behavior than any part score or single scale score by itself.

Another facet to consider in developing a frame of reference for the use of inventories centers around the extent to which the respondent is able to be candid in his answers. Some individuals find that they are not able to face the information they are revealing and are acquiring about themselves by their answers to the items. (It has been very interesting in this connection, over the twenty-five years the writer has been counseling, to note how much the completion of an inventory contributes, even before interpretation, to the insight a client achieves about his behavior and how the process helps him organize information about himself into a larger and more useful gestalt.) When the individual is unable to face these data, he distorts his responses into a picture of himself which is more acceptable to him but more confusing to the professional person working with him and trying to help him synthesize all data about his behavior. With such an individual, it is better that the counselor delay the use of inventories until, in the counselor's judgment, the client can face such data and will not need to distort his responses. This is a part of the series of decisions the counselor makes constantly about initiating procedures with clients.

Other respondents are unable to bring themselves to reveal information contained in their responses to another person. They are not sure how this other person will use the data and they fear he will judge them in some negative fashion. It is only after the relationship between client and counselor develops into mutual trust that the client begins to realize that this is one of the few situations he will ever encounter where *he* makes the judgments and is free to evaluate *his* behavior as *he* wishes. It is wiser with such a client to delay the use of inventories until such a point in the counseling relationship is reached. Then he will not need to distort his responses in order to use them as a defense against his counselor.

Still other clients want to distort results for a given purpose such as getting a job or getting into some sort of educational program, e.g., graduate school or medical school. This is probably why so many applicants to medical school score high on the scientific and social service scales of the KPR-V or why some applicants to graduate schools show extremely high L-plus-K scores.

For the reasons noted above, it seems preferable to use the results of an inventory only after the client has discussed it thoroughly with the counselor and the client knows what it is being used to accomplish. If he understands the limits within which the information will be used, the client is in a position to be more candid in his responses. If he knows there are checks on his responses which are built into an instrument like the MMPI or checks that have emerged through research on interactions between scales of the SVIB (high Group II scores and low

Group VIII scores, or vice versa), he may be less apt to try to fool himself or his counselor. This is why it seems advisable to recommend to any person about to take inventories that, even though there is no time limit, he work as rapidly as possible, because the longer he ponders an item, the less representative of his actual behavior his answer may be. If this procedure is followed, it should control as much distortion as possible because the immediate responses tend to include subliminal cues to behavior that disappear when a respondent ponders his answers.

When using the above material as a part of a professional approach to the discussion and use of personality and interest inventories, it is well to remember that there are others who confuse the issue about these structured inventories to serve their own purposes. Some persons are afraid of the information the inventories might reveal about them or about some person for whom they are responsible. Others, like Karl Menninger, have never learned to use them professionally and prefer other procedures for acquiring the same sort of information. Still others, for reasons known only to themselves, have made general attacks on the use of such inventories. In the same congressional inquiry in which Menninger testified, Karl Smith (1965) said,

> . . . I think there is now present in the American Psychological Association a very sharp and everwidening dichotomy between scientists, in which I would include myself (an industrial psychologist), and people in the testing field, including the clinical psychologists. . . . With reference to the MMPI, I would state categorically it has no theory. It is a hodgepodge of questions. This is pretty much true of all tests. This test has no theory to it. The other level of validity that you can talk about is whether the test, the MMPI, to be specific, can be, can have established for it identifiable performance criteria. I would submit that no one has yet defined any performance criteria for personality that any two clinical psychologists, and certainly any two scientifically minded psychologists, would agree upon.

Smith has presented no evidence to support his rather sweeping generalizations and his testimony should be highly questioned. In contrast to this appears the reserved and documented testimony of Brayfield (1965) as Executive Officer of the American Psychological Association and of Lebensohn (1965) as Chairman of the Public Information Committee of the American Psychiatric Association. Here are two highly respected and accredited representatives of the two appropriate major professional organizations giving testimony in agreement that structured personality inventories are worthwhile professional tools and substantial contributions to the fields of psychology and medicine.

While Brayfield's comments were made about personality inventories, much of what he says applies also to interest inventories. His comments are as follows:

> In order to minimize error and make judgment more accurate, the logic and methods of measurement have been introduced as an aid to judgment making. It is essential to recognize that *all* judgments take their point of departure from some reference point, usually an average for a known group. And judgments usually involve a statement of frequency of occurrence. . . .
>
> From this logical analysis it is only a short step to the introduction of the concept of a psychological test which is defined *as an observation of a sample of human behavior made under standard, controlled conditions which results in a linear evaluation called a score.* That is, it is systematic refinement of the normal processes of observation and evaluation. . . .
>
> Two basic considerations must obtain:
>
> First, in most instances, such tests must be supervised by a qualified psychologist.
>
> Second, in most instances, such test data must constitute only one of the sources of evaluative data. The test information must be integrated with other sources and types of data.
>
> Given these conditions, it is appropriate to consider their use with all due caution as follows:
>
> First, to identify the potentially most effective members of an occupational group. Such use assumes that it has been empirically demonstrated that scores on a personality (*or interest*) test are significantly related to some aspect of effective performance in the occupation. Example: inspectors in an electronics manufacturing company.
>
> Second, to identify members of an occupational group where it has been empirically demonstrated that the personality characteristics of its members uniquely differentiate them from members of other occupational groups or from people in general — i.e., when it has been established that the members of an occupational group have a distinctive personality profile. Example: telephone order clerks in a wholesale drug company.
>
> Third, to identify persons suitable to perform in a given situation where an analysis of the job and its setting strongly suggests that its effective performance requires certain unique personality characteristics — or contraindicates certain unique personality characteristics — and there are available measures of such personality characteristics for which there is evidence that they do indeed measure such characteristics. Example: executive vice president in a medium-sized, family owned hardware store chain.
>
> Fourth, to identify individuals suitable to perform in a given situation where an analysis of the job and its setting specifies the nature of

the performance and behavior required by the job. This further requires a well-qualified professional psychologist using a variety of sources of information, including personality tests, to formulate hypotheses regarding the potential functioning of individuals in the job and its setting. Example: the initial group of astronauts.

It should be obvious that these uses require increasing levels of competence on the part of the professional person as we go from the first to the fourth category. The last category puts a premium upon clinical judgment and professional skill and knowledge and requires the best available knowledge of the situation in which the individual applicant or employee is to perform. . . . (Brayfield, 1965)

Brayfield goes on to quote from the APA *Standards for Educational and Psychological Tests and Manuals* (1950). A more recent APA revision was published (1966a).

. . . Persons purchasing tests, assuming responsibility for testing programs, or distributing tests, should be governed by recognition of the fact that being qualified in one specialty does not necessarily result in being qualified in another specialty.

1. Being a trained psychologist does not automatically make one a qualified user of all types of psychological tests.
2. Being qualified as a user of tests in a specialty such as personnel selection, remedial reading, vocational and educational counseling, or psychodiagnosis, does not necessarily result in being qualified in any other specialty involving the use of tests. . . .

Lebensohn, as a spokesman for the American Psychiatric Association, in his agreement with Brayfield and his elaboration of the position of the American Psychiatric Association states:

Dr. Brayfield's specific recommendations about insuring a more effective use of tests in Government and safeguarding the rights of the individual employee make very good sense to us as a starting point for attacking this problem. He has emphasized the need for insuring that highly qualified staff psychologists are in charge of administering the tests with clearly defined lines of responsibility: of establishing a review procedure for personnel decisions in which test data have figured; of establishing an interagency committee to formulate guidelines for sound practices; or establishing an advisory panel to review procedures; and of setting up a task force to further the development of the science and its application in Government agencies. Although he did not mention it, I am certain he would take no exception to the proposition that members of the psychiatric profession might well be represented on some of these committees, panels, and task forces since they could bring to them the perspective of the psychiatrist who makes effective use of test results as diagnostic aids in clinical settings.

I should now like to address myself briefly to one special aspect of the problem, namely, 'invasion of privacy.' It is my impression that this problem has been a major factor in stimulating these hearings in the first place. There is, of course, no blinking the fact that the more highly developed behavioral science becomes, the more sensitive becomes the question of invasion of privacy. If we are going to find out something about human behavior that will serve to advance mankind, then obviously we have got to ask the right questions. We cannot settle for only these questions which might have been acceptable to our Victorian grandmothers. Our profession has long suffered, as this Subcommittee well knows, from an understandable but mistaken belief on the part of the public that psychiatrists do little else but pry too closely into the more intimate aspects of a patient's life, with special emphasis on his sexual habits, and religious concerns. It has been a cross for us to bear, so to speak, but we have looked upon it as an occupational hazard of psychiatric practice. It is gratifying to note, however, that the public is gradually coming to accept the fact that if a psychiatrist is to uncover pathology and embark on corrective therapy, he cannot settle for information confined to name, rank, and serial number. Fortunately, the confidentiality of information elicited in the doctor-patient relationship is reasonably well protected in our social and legal traditions — though not quite so well protected as we in psychiatry would like. Many of the states now have laws governing privileged communication which do prevent the physician and psychiatrist from divulging information about his patients without the patient's express permission. Even where such laws do not exist the patient still has the protection of a long and respected tradition, going back to Hippocrates, that the information he reveals to a physician will be held in strictest confidence.

The same degree of protection, unfortunately, does not yet pertain to Government settings wherein employees who are tested may have the test results become a matter of record. Also, there is the possibility that the test results may be used by nonprofessional persons for purposes for which they were never intended. We do have a serious problem here, and one to which I am certain this Subcommittee will address its most thoughtful consideration. However, it is one thing to take steps to protect a patient or an employee against the misuse of confidential information elicited in a test or psychiatric interview, and quite another to discourage or prohibit the professional psychiatrist or psychologist from asking the questions in the first place. I make no particular plea for any particular questions that might be asked on these tests — for that is a scientific matter for the professional workers in the field. I plead only for the principle that the questions which are asked are valid from a scientific point of view.

For example, in the *Minnesota Multiphasic Personality Inventory* test, a number of questions are asked about a person's attitude toward religion. Except for the fact that they are printed questions on a test form, they are not essentially different in their purpose from the kinds of questions that a psychiatrist might ask in more subtle ways in the course of several interviews. Gentlemen, these questions are not for the purpose of prying into a person's normal and private religious life such as whether he is a Protestant, Catholic, or Jew. What these questions seek to elicit is the presence or absence of excessive "religiosity." Excessive religiosity may severely limit a person's usefulness on a job and may be a symptom of mental illness. Our mental hospitals are filled with patients suffering from paranoid disorders who think of themselves as prophets, saints, and saviors of the world. Some of them are very kind and harmless people, but one would not want to appoint one of them as Ambassador to the Dominican Republic or as a member of the Peace Corps. It may be of special interest in this connection to note that for over 20 years the Methodist Board of Missions has made a routine use of psychiatric and psychological evaluations for all applicants for overseas service. . . .

I look upon the MMPI as simply one test. It is an important test, because it has remained in unchanged form for so many years, and therefore it has been rather standardized. I think it has a certain usefulness in mass screening because the persons who are picked up by it in my experience usually show considerable pathology.

I do not think it is a very fine screen at all. I think I would have to have many other tests and interviews to do better screening. I think that the individual questions which are asked in this test and which are taken out of context may appear to be offensive to some people because they are not understood on the entire context of the test. . . . (Lebensohn, 1965)

It can be noted readily that the preceding material deals with problems involving the invasion of privacy of the individual and the failure to maintain confidentiality of the inventory scores. This is primarily a problem when the results are used for counseling of the person who completed the inventory. A discussion of this from the standpoint of behavioral research is considered from legal and moral aspects in a paper by Ruebhausen and Brim (1966). They propose seven principles for inclusion in a general code of ethics for behavioral research, most of which also apply to any use of inventories in the schools. Their report leads to an important distinction between the two major uses of such instruments. The results tend to be more valid and usable when a client willingly takes the inventory, knowing his answers will be used to help him in his life choices. It has been demonstrated that, even when a test with as many validating scales as the MMPI is used for screening or selection, it can be distorted if the person taking the inventory wishes to do so (Cofer, 1949; Gough, 1950). Ellis (1953) has said, "In 25 studies where the ability of subjects to fake personality inventory scores was tested, it was found that they could and did fake significantly better or worse scores in 22 instances and that they did not do so in 3 instances. In several of the studies demonstrating that personality inventory scores could be faked, it was found that special detection scales, such as the F-minus-K scale of the *Minnesota Multiphasic Personality Inventory,* could partially spot and compensate for the faking." Thus, this latter use of inventories without the indices of validity possessed by the MMPI can defeat itself if the person responding wishes to distort. Most of the time, the validating scales of the MMPI used singly or in some combination will indicate how a person tried to influence unduly or distort his scores. However, most inventories do not possess the validating scales of the MMPI, and until one learns to find validating elements in terms of points of agreement within the instrument or with other sources of data, deliberate distortion by a person being tested may pass unknown.

With respect to using such devices for selection, either in a work or a school setting, even when the purpose is really to protect the individual, the validity of the devices is in question.

As Brayfield has indicated, selection of individuals for a given kind of work often requires the use of as many negative indicators as possible; that is, it is often impossible to spell out the varying combinations of characteristics which make one individual or another successful in a given job, but it is frequently possible to identify characteristics which will *prevent* a person from being successful. While he may not like this process, in the long run use of these data in selection deters him from a course of action which is usually fraught with failure. In like manner, the identification of students who need certain kinds of help to increase their chances of success in school either before they enter or after they are allowed to enter is not only a protection for them but should be considered a responsibility of the school. If the school does nothing to prevent their entry, it tacitly assumes part of the responsibility for their progress while in school. It needs to identify and to help them. As far as the material discussed here is concerned, the major concentration will be upon use of inventory scores with clients in a one-to-one setting for *their* purposes. At the same time, some material bearing on use of inventories in selection will be discussed or inferred to the school setting.

Even when used for client purposes in a school setting, it is still necessary to discuss the use of the inventory clearly and fully with the client, and with his parents if there is a legal obstacle to his giving permission to use the inventory. In the same way, it is wise to inform the school administration of the purpose of the inventories and that the instruments will not be used without securing the appropriate permission from the client or from his family. The simplest way to accomplish this is to request a note if the parent or guardian *does not* wish the inventory given.

In describing the inventory and its purpose to the client, it is customary to point out that it is used because it saves much valuable time for the counselor, it helps to check on opinions, attitudes, and interests the client has formed about himself or his environment, and it sometimes provides information that can be secured in no other way, such as that indicated earlier about the *Strong Vocational Interest Blanks* and the *Minnesota Vocational Interest Inventory.* Under ordinary circumstances, it is well to point out that the answer sheets are machine-scored and the counselor uses the scores reported by the scoring service. As indicated earlier, only in unusual circumstances, such as checking on errors or questions raised by the client about his answers to items, will the counselor refer to the way a given item is answered. In this way privacy is maintained and, if these processes are not satisfactory, the client also has the option of not completing the inventory.

If the counselor wishes to use these inventories with a client, he should take time in his structuring to be sure that the client and parents understand what is involved and what the client's choices are. The counselor should also take time to be sure his administrator understands the instruments, their purpose, and how they will be used professionally. It is also well to discuss these in appropriate public meetings so that the community can develop an *informed and knowledgeable* position about the use of such inventories.

If such steps are taken and the counselor uses these instruments cautiously and professionally, he should encounter few problems other than the unpreventable variable errors inherent in scores which represent an interaction between a client and items of an inventory. However, the importance of a *professional* frame of reference and mode of operation is vital. There are common points for all users of inventories and there are parts of this frame of reference unique to the personal and professional experience of a given counselor. It is toward enhancement of the total frame of reference that the following chapters outlining points for consideration with varying types of instruments are developed. The next points will be those pertaining to use of interest inventories in school settings.

3

....

The Counselor's Approach
to Vocational Interest Inventories

There are a number of concepts that should be kept in mind in a discussion of inventoried or measured vocational interests used in a school setting. As indicated earlier, most of these have developed around use of the two forms of the *Strong Vocational Interest Blank* with high school seniors, college students, and non-school adults, and the *Kuder Preference Record-Vocational* with both sexes from eighth grade to adults. It should be remembered that this is only one source of information about vocational interests even if it is by far the most prolific both in terms of research and in use in counseling. Other sources are statements about interests, observations of areas of manifested interest, and the relation of information about an area to interest in that area. These latter three will be given only incidental discussion when they pertain specifically to use of a given inventory.

Interest inventories are ordinarily considered as attempts to quantify interests or provide a score which describes a client's feelings of like or dislike, sometimes called acceptance-rejection reactions, to varied subjective areas of interest. As Cottle and Downie (1960) point out, there are divergent viewpoints on what these measurements represent and how vocational interests develop. Regardless of controversy, a series of assumptions or hypotheses have emerged from the use of vocational interest inventories with clients and from research projects. The pertinent ones for counselor consideration are discussed below.

The first of these is an elaboration and re-emphasis of the acceptance-rejection proposition stated by Fryer (1931). At first, attention was devoted only to the acceptance aspect of this statement and the counselor then tended to focus on the interpretation of high scores. In recent years, however, with increasing empirical and statistical evidence mounting on the value of interpreting scores in terms of patterns of high *and* low scores, more attention has been given to the interaction of acceptance *and* rejection scores in interest measurement. Kuder (1946) published patterns or profiles of scores for various occupational groups in his manual for the KPR-V, Form B. It is obvious from an inspection of these group profiles that low scores can be as important in describing occupational groups as can high scores. An example of this from empirical observation is the tendency of mechanics and various types of engineers who score high on the Mechanical and Scientific Scales of the KPR-V to score low on the Literary Scale. In like manner, Strong's (1955) findings that low scores on the SVIB were the most stable over a period of years also lends research support to this concept. Empirical evidence is found for this on the SVIB in the tendency for individuals with high scores on the occupational groups in the sciences (Groups I and II) to obtain low scores in the business area (Groups VIII and IX). Later in the chapter, correlational data will also be presented in support of this hypothesis. It is also supported by the finding of bipolar factors representing Science vs. Business in factor analyses carried out on the SVIB by Strong (1943) and Thurstone (Super & Crites, 1962) and on the SVIB and KPR-V by Cottle (1950) and D'Arcy (1954). This broadens the approach to interpreting interest scores as well as providing an internal check on the profile of a given client on these inventories. This topic will be considered further in this chapter when the intercorrelations of scores within the scales of the SVIB and KPR-V and between these two inventories are discussed, because the intercorrelations emphasize the positive *and* negative relationships between the various scales.

It is obvious that the approach taken in construction of interest inventories by asking an individual to answer most *and* least liked to the content of an item or to mark it like or dislike will tend to produce high *and* low scores as discussed above. It is less obvious, however, that such a procedure is asking him to make a choice which will be his self-estimate of his feelings, emotions, and attitudes toward these items which represent stimuli related to vocational activities, situations, or to people of various sorts. The attempt to quantify such feelings has led to the questions about the interpretation of interest inventory scores.

How stable are an individual's responses to such items? The limited studies of the stability or permanence of interest scores over a considerable period of time, such as Strong's *Vocational Interests 18 Years After College* (1955) and publications dealing with test-retest scores over several years or empirical observations of those in counseling, lead one to believe that scores for the average college-bound student remain fairly stable over a considerable period of time. Only limited information is available at this point on the non-college student (Kuder, 1966; Clark and Campbell, 1965). Perhaps as Bordin (1943) has suggested, these reactions are an expression of the client's self-concept, and to the extent that this remains relatively stable, the scores will tend to repeat themselves rather closely over a period of time. Perhaps, also, this is why the literature has considered interests as crystallizing toward the end of adolescence. The end of adolescence may be the point where the client's search for self crystallizes to a sufficiently permanent state that reflections of it in interest inventory scores are also more permanent.

One hears questions also about whether inventory scores are a function of the instrument and its construction or whether they are a reflection of attributes of the individual who responds to the items. The answer appears to be that they are the results of the *interaction* of the individual *and* the inventory and cannot be considered separately in any way. To the extent that the client has responded candidly to these items, they reflect his attitude toward the material they contain. If the material reflects the interests of physicians, his interests as shown by a high score are to that extent like physicians. If the material represents mechanical activities, his high score represents a high degree of interest in the mechanical area, or his low score the reverse. The scores cannot be inferred to other material unless research or empirical evidence has shown there is a relationship. For example, in a study of 400 adult male World War II veterans by Cottle (1950a) the correlation between the Mf scale on the MMPI and the MF scale of the SVIB-M was −.41; that between the MF scale of the SVIB-M and the MF score on the KPR-V was .63 (Form B of the Kuder has a series of weights developed by discriminant analysis for the nine scales, which produces an MF score); and that between the Mf scale of the MMPI and the KPR-V was −.03. It would appear from these limited data that the MMPI and KPR-V scores for masculinity-femininity are measuring nothing in common, while the SVIB score is measuring something in common with each of the other two scales. (It should be remembered that this masculinity-femininity score is confusing because its poles are reversed from inventory to inventory. On the MMPI, a high score for males represents femininity; that for females represents masculinity. On the SVIB-M a high score represents masculinity and on the SVIB-W it represents femininity. On the Guilford-Zimmerman Temperament Survey (GZTS), there are different columns in the profile and the meanings of a high score are in the direction of the sex of the person taking the inventory. This is further complicated by the general tendency discussed earlier for the counselor to interpret masculinity as an interest in things, processes, and non-linguistic or non-word symbols and femininity as an interest in people, language, and communication. However, the Mf scale of the MMPI contains three major groups of items: those dealing with people vs. things, those dealing with an interest in cultural pursuits, and those dealing with homosexuality.) While discussing MF scales, it should be pointed out that the correlation in Cottle's study (1949), as shown in Table 3, between SVIB-M MF scales and the KPR-V Mechanical scale was .68, so an approximation of MF for the KPR-V could be made from the Mechanical scale score. From these examples, it should be clear that scales named the same on different inventories cannot be considered to have the same meaning unless statistical research and empirical evidence have shown they do.

Recent research has focused attention on the amount of response set involved in the score on scales of various inventories. Fredericksen (1965) says, "Interpretations of the correlations of set scores with inventory scores are thus confused not only by possible confounding of set and content in inventory scores but also by different possible cause and effect relationships and by different possible perceptions of what is desirable." One way to explore response set on the SVIB is to mark three separate answer sheets: one all *Like,* one all *Indifferent,* and one all *Dislike.* If this is done for the SVIB-M it produces the scores shown below. Only the significantly high (T = 40 or more) and low (T = 10 or less) scores are shown for the SVIB-M marked all *Like:*

High	*High*	*Low*
Osteopath	Accountant	Artist
Production Manager	Office Manager	Mathematician
Math.-Phys. Sci. Tchr.	Mortician	Physicist
Printer	Pharmacist	
Policeman	Life Ins. Salesman	
YMCA Phys. Director	Int. Maturity	
Personnel Director	Occup. Level	
Public Administrator	Specialization Level	
YMCA Secretary	Masculinity-Femininity	
H.S. Soc. Sci. Tchr.	(Salesmanager and Real	
Social Worker	Estate Salesman are	
Minister	just below the significant	
Senior CPA	level.)	

It is difficult to perceive whether this result of marking all items *Like* is just a function of the construction of the SVIB-M or an actual part of a series of patterns for those occupations marked "High." Perhaps an occupational characteristic of men in these occupations is to like more things than they dislike. The concern of the counselor at this point is to know what proportion of responses on an answer sheet were marked *L.* From this, he can see how much effect this response set had in helping to produce any of the acceptable interest scores listed "High" above. Not enough research has been done to know whether it is possible to get high scores on those occupational scales without a preponderance of *Like* responses.

When an SVIB-M answer sheet is marked all *Indifferent,* the following results occur:

High	*High*	*Low*
Farmer	H.S. Soc. Sci. Tchr.	Pres. Mfg. Concern
Aviator	Musician Performer	
Carpenter	Senior CPA	
Printer	Office Man	
Math.-Phys. Sci. Tchr.	Interest Maturity	
Voc. Ag. Tchr.	Masculinity-Femininity	
Policeman		
Forest Service		
YMCA Secretary		

Again, it is important for the counselor to know the proportion of *Indifferent* responses on an answer sheet in order to estimate the effect of this response set on scores in the occupational groups listed above.

When an SVIB-M answer sheet is marked all *Dislike,* the following results appear:

High	*Low*	*Low*
Real Estate Salesman	Psychologist	All Group V
Advertising Man	Veterinarian	occupations
Lawyer	Aviator	Senior CPA
Author-Journalist	Carpenter	Accountant
Pres. Mfg. Concern	Printer	Office Man
Occupational Level	Policeman	
(Just below significant level	Math.-Phys. Sci. Tchr.	
are Architect, Life Ins.	Industrial Arts Tchr.	
Salesman, Specialization	Voc. Ag. Tchr.	
Level, Interest Maturity,	Policeman	
and Masculinity-Femininity.)	Forest Service	

It can be seen from the results above that marking SVIB-M items all *Dislike,* in converse to the other two responses, produces more low scores than high scores, particularly in Groups IV and V. The high scores occur in Groups IX, X, XI and Occupational Level.

Counselors have wondered why so many SVIB-M profiles show high scores for Printer, Policeman, H. S. Math Sci. Tchr., H. S. Soc. Sci. Tchr., Senior CPA, Office Man, Interest Maturity and Masculinity-Femininity. The results reported indicate this probably occurs because of a preponderance of *Like* and *Indifferent* responses over *Dislike* responses. The occupational scales listed as having high scores from either *L* or *I* responses are also the ones with the highest chance score possibility (shaded area on the profile, Figure 1). While Farmer and Real Estate Salesman are not in this list, they do have high chance score possibilities. Real Estate Salesman probably because any preponderance of *L* and *D* responses produces a high score. It appears then that this response set result explains the majority of high "chance scores" on the SVIB-M. In like manner, few *Indifferent* responses may produce high scores on Real Estate Salesman, Life Ins. Salesman and Occupational Level. Almost any combination of *L, I,* and *D* responses seems to produce a high score on Specialization Level and may account for the limited use this scale has had.

The SVIB-M scales where a high score is *not* produced by response set in any one direction and therefore are probably true occupational scores are: Psychologist, Physician, Dentist, Veterinarian, Mathematician, Physicist, Engineer, Chemist, City School Superintendent, and Purchasing Agent.

Similar results occur when the SVIB-W answer sheet is marked all *L, I,* or *D.* For example, marking all items *Like* has the following results:

High	*High*	*Low*
Social Worker	Home Econ. Tchr.	Librarian
Lawyer	Dietician	
Housewife	Nurse	
Elem. Tchr.	Lab. Technician	
Office Worker	Physical Therapist	
Stenog.-Sec.	Femininity-Masculinity	
Bus. Ed. Tchr.		

When all items are marked *Indifferent,* the following results appear:

High	*High*	*Low*
Housewife	Math-Phys. Sci. Tchr.	Author
Office Worker	Lab. Technician	
Stenog.-Sec.	Physical Therapist	
Bus. Ed. Tchr.	Engineer	
Phys. Ed. Tchr.	Femininity-Masculinity	
Occupational Therapist		

FIGURE 1

Special SVIB profile sheet developed at the University of Kansas Guidance Bureau.

GB FORM 30
REVISED 1958

Report on Vocational Interest Blank for Men

Name _____ Age ___ Date _____ School _____ Case no. ___

Group	Occupation	Raw Score	Standard Score	C							B−	B	B+	A			
				0	5	10	15	20	25	30	35	40	45	50	55	60	65
I				−195	−170	−135	−110	−85	−60	−35	−10	15	45	70	95	120	
	Artist			−260	−220	−180	−130	−90	−40	0	45	90	130	180	220	265	
	Psychologist (rev.)			−140	−115	−90	−60	−30	0	25	50	80	105	130	160	185	
	Architect			−125	−100	−75	−50		0	25	50	75	100	125	150	175	
	Physician (rev.)			−75	−60	−47	−25	−10	7	25	42	60	75	93	110	127	
	Dentist			−85	−70	−50	−35	−17	0	18	35	50	70	85	103	120	
II				−105	−90	−75	−60	−45	−25		20	40	60	85	105	125	
	Chemist			−110	−85	−65	−45	−25	−5	20	40	60	80	100	123	145	
	Mathematician			−175	−140	−105	−70	−35	0	35	70	100	140	170	210	240	
	Engineer			−103	−80	−60	−40	−20	0	20	45	65	90	110	130	150	
III	Production Manager			−95	−80	−62	−47	−32	−17	−2	15	30	45	60	75	90	
IV	Farmer			−150	−130	−105	−85	−65	−45	−25	−5	15	35	55	75	95	
	Math. Sci. Teacher			−165	−140	−110	−85	−60	−30	−5	20	45	75	100	125	155	
	Forest Service			−60	−43	−28	−6	15	33	50	70	88	105	125	145	163	
	Army Officer			−85	−60	−35	−10	15	40	65	88	110	135	160	185	205	
	Aviator			−135	−110	−85	−60	−36	−10	14	35	60	85	110	135	160	
V				−185	−160	−135	−110	−85	−60	−35	−10	15	40	65	90	110	
	Y.M.C.A. Phys. Dir.			−125	−100	−75	−50	−20	5	30	55	80	110	135	160	185	
	Personnel Manager			−83	−65	−50	−35	−20	−5	10	25	43	58	73	88	103	
	Vocational Counselor			−180	−150	−125	−95	−65	−35	−5	25	60	90	120	150	180	
	Soc. Sci. Teacher			−145	−120	−100	−75	−50	−25	0	20	45	70	95	115	140	
	City School Supt.			−75	−55	−35	−14	3	20	40	60	80	100	120	138	158	
	Minister			−140	−110	−85	−55	−25	5	35	65	95	125	150	180	210	
	Social Worker			−180	−140	−110	−80	−40	−10	25	60	95	130	160	200	230	
VI	Musician			−125	−107	−90	−70	−55	−35	−20	0	17	35	52	70	90	
	Music Performer			−155	−135	−110	−80	−57	−35	−10	10	35	55	80	100	125	
	Music Teacher			−140	−110	−85	−60	−30	−5	20	50	75	100	130	155	180	
VII	C.P.A. Partner			−72	−60	−45	−37	−17	−5	10	25	40	52	67	80	95	
VIII				−82	−72	−60	−47	−37	−25	−12	0	12	25	37	50	62	
	Senior C.P.A.			−130	−105	−80	−55	−35	−12	10	30	50	70	90	110	130	
	Junior Accountant			−80	−65	−57	−42	−27	−7	7	20	35	50	65	80	95	
	Office Worker			−115	−97	−80	−65	−45	−30	−12	5	22	40	55	72	90	
	Purchasing Agent			−80	−67	−52	−37	−25	−10	5	20	35	50	62	77	92	
	Banker			−125	−105	−85	−67	−50	−30	−10	10	30	50	67	87	105	
	Pharmacist			−105	−92	−70	−55	−37	−20	−5	12	27	45	60	77	95	
IX				−160	−140	−120	−100	−75	−55	−35	−12	10	30	50	75	95	
	Sales Manager			−110	−97	−75	−55	−35	−15	2	20	40	60	77	95	115	
	Real Estate Slsmn.			−190	−165	−140	−115	−92	−70	−45	−23	0	25	45	70	92	
	Life Insurance Slsmn.			−165	−140	−117	−90	−65	−40	−15	10	35	60	80	105	130	
X				−270	−240	−205	−175	−140	−110	−75	−45	−10	20	55	85	120	
	Advertising Man			−195	−170	−145	−115	−85	−60	−30	0	30	60	85	115	145	
	Lawyer			−140	−115	−90	−70	−45	−25	0	20	45	65	90	110	135	
	Author-Journalist			−400	−340	−280	−230	−170	−120	−60	−10	40	100	150	200	260	
XI	President (Mfg. Conc.)			−85	−70	−55	−40	−27	−12	0	15	27	42	55	70	85	
	Occupational Level																
	Masculinity-Femininity																
	Interest Maturity																

When all items are marked *Dislike*, the following results occur:

High	*Low*	*Low*
Artist	Social Worker	Occupational Therapist
Author	Soc. Sci. Tchr.	Nurse
Librarian	YWCA Secretary	Musician Tchr.
Physician	Home Econ. Tchr.	Physical Therapist
Femininity-Masculinity	Phys. Ed. Tchr. (college)	Engineer

The SVIB-W scales which show high scores *not* affected by a preponderance of any one response are:

English Teacher   Buyer
Psychologist   Dentist
Soc. Sci. Tchr.   Musician Tchr.
YWCA Sec.   Musician Performer
Life Ins. Saleswoman

Counselors have wondered why most women get high scores on Housewife, Office Worker, Stenographer-Secretary, and Business Education Teacher. The terms "prior-to-marriage occupations," "general feminine interests," and "non-career occupations" have been used to explain that these are temporary occupations for many women. The real explanation of these frequent high scores for most women is the preponderance of any combination of *Like* and *Indifferent* responses over *Dislike* responses. The same condition produces high scores on Laboratory Technician and Physical Therapist, while a preponderance of *Dislike* and *Indifferent* responses over *Like* responses produces a high score on the Femininity pole of the Femininity-Masculinity Scale.

Obviously no one answers these inventories all *L*, all *I*, or all *D*, but if the counselor is to make any interpretation of the scores on scales affected by such a response set tendency he must know the proportion of *L*, *I*, and *D* responses among the total number of items. *This count of each kind of possible response should be made a standard part of the scoring of all personality and interest inventories.*

Although many persons working with interest inventories are inclined to discount the effect of emotions on stability of scores, strong emotions not really related to the interest area can introduce bias into interpretation of scores. Whether this is a reaction against teaching and other helping occupations by an adolescent who has strong feelings about the life a parent leads as a teacher, or whether it is a product of pronounced maladjustment requiring intensive psychotherapy, the reaction can distort the scores of the client on an inventory. Unless the counselor is aware of this condition in the client and interprets the client's scores and other data with extreme caution, he can harm the client more than he helps him. An example of this would be the caution needed in interpreting very high or very low scores on the Persuasive or Social Service scales of the KPR-V. These may be perfectly representative of high scores of a client who is very outgoing and relates well to people or the low scores of a client who is interested in research or mechanical activities requiring very little contact with or interest in people. On the other hand, the extremely high scores on these two scales may be reflecting the client who is unable to be alone and needs help in changing this behavior before he can show a real vocational interest pattern. The client with extremely low scores may be indicating pronounced withdrawal tendencies rather than an actual vocational interest pattern. Until the counselor has data other than the inventory scores to check this, he should discuss the scores cautiously with the client or even refrain from discussing them.

The average correlation between scores on interest inventories and indices of ability and aptitude is between .30 and .40. This means that these inventory scores, while showing more than a chance relationship, are of limited value in predicting cognitive skills and vice versa. Hence the fact that a client gets a standard score of 750 on the math part of the College Entrance Examination Scholastic Aptitude Test may not mean that he will be interested in academic areas dependent on such proficiency. The counselor should always bear in mind that innate potential does not automatically produce interest in that area, rather it is the reverse. Interest will more frequently cause a client to investigate how he can develop his aptitudes in that area.

Most of the research on the meaning of inventory scores has been conducted on samples of college-bound populations. This means roughly the top third to top half of general population and may tell very little about the meaning of those inventories for use with non-college persons. Recent emphasis on hard-core unemployed, non-white minority groups and noncollege-bound youth in general has caused administrators and counselors to take another look at the results of the counseling program to date. Particularly on the East Coast and the West Coast, primary counseling emphasis has been on college placement, with only a limited effort made in counseling or placement of the noncollege student by the school. With the advent of inventories like the *Minnesota Vocational Interest Inventory* and government and private emphasis on job placement for noncollege groups, the counselor will have to replan his use of inventories with his clients and learn new skills with these newer inventories. As he does this he should also plan research to highlight results of the newer approach in order to see what he is accomplishing and be able to justify his new program in his community. Where possible, he should plan his program so it dovetails with that being carried on by the State Employment Service to avoid duplication of effort and produce a stronger program through this broader application. Finances available from government and private sources for organizing programs and for research on newer approaches can be utilized as another source of gathering knowledge about the meaning of vocational interest inventory scores with noncollege groups.

Information secured from interest inventories tends to supplement that secured from personality inventories and to serve as validation of scores on the latter instruments, if the counselor knows how to do this. At first consideration, interest and personality inventories show quite limited correlations as evidenced by information from Cottle's (1949) correlations for the MMPI, SVIB-M, KPR-V, and *Bell Adjustment Inventory* in Tables 3 and 4. However, this is the result of reduced relationships when a heterogeneous group of 400 adult males is used as the sample on whom these correlations are secured. In this situation, the general mixture within the group tends to cancel out or lower relationships which can be demonstrated when the sample is selected on a given criterion. Thus when Cottle and Powell (1949) chose members from the original group who manifested scores above T-equals-55 and below T-equals-45 on the Mf scale of the MMPI, tests of significance indicated relationships among scales of the four inventories which centered about people versus non-people-related behavior. This seems to offer the possibility that when a given criterion of behavior is used as the basis for choosing a sample and the members of the sample are given inventories whose scales offer the possibility of relationships, it will be possible to demonstrate that aspects of behavior manifested by such scores are related and support each other in describing client behavior. For example, if scores above and below selected points on the Social Introversion scale of the MMPI were used as the criterion for selecting the sample, one might expect the Mf, Pa, and possibly the Sc to show differences on the MMPI. This same criterion might show significant differences on people-oriented versus non-people-oriented scales of other personality and interest inventories, such as the Group V and IX occupational scales of the SVIB-M or the Persuasive, Literary, and Social Service scales of the KPR-V. As the counselor learns to look for such relationships, the personality and interest inventory scores or profiles take on a more complex but more complete meaning for him, and his interpretations to his clients are more real and effective.

For example, Table 4 showing the correlation of SVIB-M and KPR-V scores with MMPI scores of 400 adult males (Cottle, 1949) and the part of Table 3 which shows correlation of *Bell Adjustment Inventory* scores with SVIB-M and KPR-V scores of the same group indicate very limited and low or low-moderate relationship between the scores of personality

TABLE 3

Correlation of SVIB-M and KPR-V Scores with MMPI Scores of 400 Adult Males (Cottle, 1949)

TEST		Strong Voc. Interest Blank									Kuder Preference Record									
		I	II	V	VIII	IX	X	IM	OL	MF	M	C	S	P	A	L	M	SS	Cl	Mf
		12	13	14	15	16	17	18	19	20	21	22	23	24	25	26	27	28	29	30
L	1	-.04	-.03	.08	.00	-.05	-.01	.04	-.06	-.04	-.03	.03	.04	-.03	-.03	.04	-.01	.09	.02	-.06
F	2	.14	.04	-.08	-.12	-.02	.14	-.14	.01	-.13	-.05	.00	-.06	-.07	.13	.10	.14	-.06	-.05	-.08
Hs	3	.04	.01	-.11	.03	-.01	-.02	-.10	-.04	-.04	.05	.03	-.04	-.03	.09	-.07	.01	.01	.04	-.04
D	4	.17	.03	-.17	-.01	-.13	.10	-.15	-.08	-.14	.02	.05	-.03	-.13	.17	.00	.02	-.09	.09	-.14
Hy	5	.02	-.08	.03	-.01	.01	.05	.03	.00	-.11	-.03	-.05	-.06	.02	.01	.02	.05	.08	-.03	-.04
Pd	6	.06	-.01	-.05	-.07	.01	.15	-.06	-.06	-.09	-.03	-.04	-.04	-.05	.06	.04	.17	-.03	-.01	-.09
Mf	7	.15	.13	.21	-.14	-.03	.25	.09	-.04	-.41	-.30	-.11	-.24	-.07	.03	.24	.35	-.01	.03	-.03
Pa	8	.16	.07	.02	-.11	-.08	.06	.00	-.06	-.14	-.06	-.05	.03	-.13	.05	.04	.17	-.02	-.01	-.16
Pt	9	.19	.07	-.20	-.08	-.09	.06	-.22	-.14	-.12	.00	.04	-.05	-.17	.17	-.07	.15	-.12	.09	-.17
Sc	10	.18	.06	-.14	-.09	-.07	.07	-.14	-.07	-.09	.01	-.01	-.02	-.15	.11	-.04	.14	-.07	.02	-.13
Ma	11	-.04	-.02	.02	.00	.13	.00	.07	.00	-.02	-.01	-.10	-.07	.05	.00	-.02	.09	.03	-.07	.02

Minn. Multiphasic

40

TABLE 4
Intercorrelation of SVIB-M and KPR-V Scores and Correlations Between SVIB-M, KPR-V and Bell Adjustment Inventory Scores for 400 Adult Males (Cottle, 1949)

		Strong Voc. Interest Blank									Kuder Preference Record										Bell Adj. Inv.			
TEST		I	II	V	VIII	IX	X	IM	OL	MF	M	C	S	P	A	L	M	SS	Cl	Mf	Ho	He	So	Em
		12	13	14	15	16	17	18	19	20	21	22	23	24	25	26	27	28	29	30	31	32	33	34
I	12		.61	−.25	−.76	−.59	.26	−.40	−.01	−.09	.17	−.25	.34	−.64	.45	.07	.18	−.11	−.47	−.26	.09	.01	.23	.14
II	13			−.39	−.34	−.72	−.23	−.24	−.11	.39	.58	.14	.67	−.61	.29	−.22	−.15	−.28	−.29	.19	.00	−.03	.18	.05
V	14				−.06	.10	.02	.70	−.14	−.31	−.43	−.26	−.45	.20	−.15	.30	.20	.39	−.11	−.26	−.08	−.04	−.35	−.19
VIII	15					.39	−.38	.19	−.11	.17	.02	.50	−.20	.36	−.29	−.22	−.16	−.43	.60	.25	−.02	.05	.00	.06
IX	16						.34	.12	.39	−.32	−.44	−.36	−.75	.70	−.32	.13	.11	.04	.29	−.14	−.01	−.03	−.28	−.11
X	17							−.23	.47	−.56	−.63	−.26	−.33	.07	.01	.48	.36	.12	−.03	−.52	.06	−.01	−.04	.00
IM	18								.01	−.06	−.44	−.10	−.09	.10	−.33	.17	−.06	−.07	−.01	.03	−.06	−.04	−.34	−.21
OL	19									−.29	−.39	−.16	−.11	.10	−.30	−.17	−.23	.02	.05	−.02	−.01	−.07	−.19	−.14
MF	20										.68	.20	.44	−.24	−.28	−.49	−.43	−.41	−.10	.63	−.07	−.04	.02	−.04
M	21											.07	.49	−.24	.25	−.47	−.36	−.31	−.25	.65	−.02	.04	.13	.05
C	22												.24	−.10	−.25	−.12	−.22	−.31	.53	.28	.02	.02	.12	.05
S	23													−.44	−.03	−.35	−.29	−.10	−.27	.31	−.08	−.11	.10	−.04
P	24														−.28	.07	−.07	.12	.21	.33	−.10	−.05	−.33	−.19
A	25															−.17	.07	−.28	−.33	−.21	.07	.06	.18	.14
L	26																.19	−.05	.03	−.28	−.03	.01	−.13	−.11
M	27																	−.04	−.05	−.44	.12	.11	.06	.19
SS	28																		.24	−.26	−.06	−.10	−.22	−.19
Cl	29																			−.20	.05	.09	.12	.13
Mf	30																				−.09	−.04	−.15	−.15

Strong = rows 12–20. Kuder Pref. Rec. = rows 21–30.

41

inventories and interest inventories. For a sample of 400, a correlation of .13 is a significant departure from a chance relationship and, while there are 26 of these (out of a possible 99) between the MMPI and the SVIB-M, only the highest five are between .20 and .41. There are 20 significant correlations between the MMPI and the KPR-V out of a possible 110, but only four of these range between .20 and the highest, .35. In contrast, when one looks at the correlations between the SVIB-M and KPR-V shown in Table 3 and the correlations between the MMPI and the Bell A.I. shown in Table 6 they appear considerably higher. In Table 3, the two interest inventories show 55 correlations out of a possible 90 between .20 and .75 with 17 between .45 and .75. In Table 5, the two personality inventories show 32 out of a possible 44 between .20 and .78 with seven between .45 and .78.

These data support the use of both interest and personality inventories in counseling because of the very limited overlap in measurement.

However, if one looks at the highest correlations between the interest inventories and the personality inventories, they hint at relationships which would probably be considerably higher if a more homogeneous group were selected. Three of the five highest correlations between the MMPI and the SVIB-M are for the MMPI Mf scale and the SVIB-M Social Welfare (Group V), Linguistic (Group X), and Masculinity-Femininity scales. The other two are between the MMPI Pt scale and the SVIB-M Social Welfare and Interest Maturity Scales. All five of these seem to center around relationships with people, but it is difficult to interpret the reason for or the effect of the Pt scale in this grouping.

In the case of the highest correlations between the MMPI and the KPR-V, all four are between the MMPI Mf scale and the KPR-V Mechanical and Scientific (negative), Literary and Musical (positive) scales. Again the focus is on relationships with people or linguistic-nonlinguistic activities.

In contrast to the above discussion of limited correlations between personality inventories and interest inventories, when one observes the relationships shown between scales within each interest inventory and between the scales of the two interest inventories as discussed above in connection with Table 3, a different picture emerges.

The scales of the interest inventories which one logically expects to be correlated within each instrument and between the instruments show such a relationship. In the case of correlations between the two interest inventories, the relationships emerge in spite of the fact that the two instruments were constructed quite differently and for somewhat different purposes.

Within the SVIB-M itself, the Scientific scales (Group I) are highly related in a positive way to the Technical-Scientific scales (Group II) and have high negative relationship to the Business Detail scales (Group VIII) and the Business Contact scales (Group IX). This supports the empirical observation that persons in business tend to reject the science areas or vice versa. It is further supported by the high negative correlation ($-.72$) between the Group II scales (Mathematician, Engineer, and Chemist) and the Group IX scales (Sales Manager, Real Estate Salesman, and Insurance Salesman). The correlation of .70 between the Social Welfare scales (Group V) and the Interest Maturity Scale bears out a phenomenon usually observed that these scales move upward or downward together. In the case of both the Science versus Business phenomenon and that for Social Welfare and Interest Maturity the relationship offers the counselor two places to check accuracy of scoring for the SVIB-M. Likewise, the moderately high relationships between the Linguistic scales (Group X) and the Occupational Level and Masculinity-Femininity Scales (.47 and $-.56$, respectively) offer a further check for the counselor on the scoring of the instrument. In this latter case, it also focuses on the "people-related activities" meaning usually inferred from these scales.

The correlations among the scales of the KPR-V itself show similar but lower relationships. This occurs because the process Kuder used in constructing the inventory produced lower intercorrelations among these scales. He chose items which had a high correlation with each other for a given scale and which minimized the correlation of each item with items in other scales. In spite of this process, the KPR-V Mechanical, Scientific, and Masculinity-Femininity scales show a moderate positive relationship with each other and a moderate negative relationship with the Literary scale. This is more support for the empirically observed "Things vs. People" phenomenon and again points toward the high and low patterns of scores expected on these scales with persons wanting to be mechanics and engineers. Another pattern of scores found in these correlations is that represented by the correlation of .53 between the Computational and Clerical scales (the business detail pattern). The negative correlation of $-.44$ between Scientific and Persuasive scales again emphasizes this inverse relationship also found in the SVIB-M correlations discussed above. One more bit of support for the Linguistic-Nonlinguistic patterns mentioned previously in discussion of the MMPI, SVIB-M and KPR-V correlations is the negative correlation of $-.44$ between the Kuder Musical scale and the Kuder Masculinity-Femininity scale. It should be noted that KPR-V Masculinity-Femininity scores are a function of discriminant weights among the nine scales and thus meaning of this correlation is not clear.

In a discussion of the correlations between the scales of the SVIB-M and those of the KPR-V attention should be focused on the logical relationships that emerge even though the instruments were not originally intended to produce these relationships. The KPR-V Mechanical scale shows moderately high positive relationships with the SVIB-M Group II and Masculinity-Femininity scores and negative relationships with Groups V, IX, Interest Maturity and Occupational Level. That is, when the Mechanical scale is high, so are the Mathematician, Chemist, Engineer, and Masculinity scales of the SVIB-M, and the scores on SVIB scales for occupations relating to people and activities of a linguistic nature are low. The Business Detail occupations of the Strong are moderately (.50) related to the Computational Scale of the Kuder. When the Scientific Scale of the Kuder is high, so are the Group II and Masculinity Scales of the Strong, while Strong scores for Group V and IX are low. Again this is support for a linguistic (people) or a non-linguistic (science) pattern of scores on these inventories. If the Persuasive Scale of the Kuder is high, the Strong scores for Business Contact are high and those for Groups I and II (Science) are low. The single moderately high correlation between the Kuder Artistic Scale and Group I on the Strong could be anticipated because Group I contains Artist and Architect occupational scales. The Kuder Literary Scale has a moderate positive correlation with Strong Group X and a moderate negative correlation with the SVIB Masculinity-Femininity Scale. As found with the KPR-V intercorrelations, the only significant correlation of the Kuder Musical Scale was −.43 with the Strong. The Kuder Social Service scale shows a low moderate positive correlation with Strong Group V scores and low moderate negative correlation with Strong Groups VIII and Masculinity-Femininity. The Kuder Clerical scale shows a negative correlation with Strong Group I and, what might be anticipated, a positive correlation of .60 with Strong Business Detail scores. This may be the basis for a separate "Business Detail versus Science" factor in addition to the more general "Business versus Science" factor which also included business contact elements. The statistically derived Kuder Masculinity-Femininity Scale has a negative correlation of −.52 with the SVIB Group X scores and a positive correlation of .63 with the Strong Masculinity-Femininity Scale.

The relationships above are the reasons for the statement that certain logical associations between the scales of these two instruments are to be expected and that when they do not emerge in counseling, the counselor should look first for inaccuracy in scoring of one or both inventories. The counselor familiar with such relationships can synthesize case data more effectively and provide a more meaningful interpretation of the scores and the synthesized data to a client.

This first part of the chapter has considered ways in which the counselor's use of interest inventories with clients or for research can offer a richer experience and development for the counselor, a growth of knowledge about the interrelationships of selected scales on various inventories, and a more meaningful interpretation of these scores to clients. The balance of the chapter considers the historical development of the area of vocational interest measurement.

The Development of Interest Inventories

Probably the first significant attempts to inventory vocational interests grew out of a seminar held under the leadership of Yoakum at Carnegie Institute of Technology in 1919. The efforts of members of this seminar to quantify vocational interests in academic and business settings is described in Fryer's work, *The Measurement of Interests in Relation to Human Adjustment* (1931). This text is an excellent summary of the work in the area of vocational interest measurement to 1930. While few modern students of this topic appear to have read Fryer's work, it is worthwhile to peruse because he seems to have anticipated and indicated most of the major problems encountered in the measurement of interests to the present time. He points toward two approaches to measuring vocational interests. The subjective approach using self-rating or self-report blanks like the current inventories and the objective appoach using information tests, learning and distraction tests, and association tests.

The second major point in this area was the development of the *Strong Vocational Interest Blanks* for Men and for Woman which is described in Strong's volume, *Vocational Interests of Men and Women* (1943). While much of Strong's discussion of the research in the area of inventoried vocational interests naturally centers about the SVIB with which he began working in 1927, he covers most of the research from 1930 to 1942. The SVIB was used widely with college students and adults and a tremendous amount of research was conducted with this inventory. Until his death in 1963, Strong administered a research institute and depository for materials on the SVIB at Stanford. Since then the major center for research on the SVIB has been maintained at the University of Minnesota.

In the 1930's, Kuder began developing Form A of the KPR-V at Ohio State. This first form had seven scales, Form B had nine scales, and Form C has ten scales. Form E has been developed specifically for use with junior and senior high school students. This inventory, as indicated earlier, was created by item analysis techniques to measure interest in various kinds of activities. It is only by other research and by use in counseling that the scores on this inventory can be inferred to occupations. Kuder has since developed Form D and Form DD which use occupational criterion groups similar to those of the SVIB, but the statistical development and interpretation are different from that of the SVIB.

In 1931, Allport and Vernon published a *Study of Values*. It has been widely used in counseling college students and was revised as the Allport-Vernon-Lindzey *Study of Values* (1951). It covers six areas of values which are related to academic and vocational choices. These are based on Spranger's types and are titled: Theoretical, Economic, Aesthetic, Social, Political, and Religious values. Research has indicated that this inventory will differentiate among college students in various curricula.

In 1940, Lee and Thorpe published the *Occupational Interest Inventory,* often referred to as the California Interest Inventory.

Carter (1940) has done considerable research in the area of vocational interests, most of it centering around the concept that choice of a vocation is a practical adjustment to the individual's environment. Darley (1941) in his *Clinical Aspects and Interpretation of the Strong Vocational Interest Blank* proposed that occupational interests are by-products of personality development. He later modified this concept in his 1955 publication. Bordin (1943) suggested in his publication on vocational interests that, "in answering a Strong Vocational Interest Test an individual is expressing his acceptance of a particular view or concept of himself in terms of occupational stereotypes." Super (1949) criticizes previous writers and proposes, "Interests are a product of interaction between inherited aptitudes and endocrine factors, on the one hand, and opportunity and social evaluation on the other." All of these writers, including Super, point in various ways to the fact that the development of vocational interests is a part of the overall development of the individual which seems to crystallize, as Strong (1943) puts it, somewhere in the period between age 15 and age 25 and remain relatively stable from age 25, subject to natural changes and limitations as a function of aging. Terman (1954) has also pointed out that some types of vocational interest, particularly those based in the sciences, manifest themselves much earlier than others (ages 10 to 12), while vocational interests based on the humanities and social sciences crystallize much later.

Darley and Hagenah (1955) in Chapter V of *Vocational Interest Measurement* summarize the research basic to these theories very comprehensively. Perhaps one of the most succinct summaries of vocational interest measurement theory to that time was written by Hahn and MacLean (1955). They state:

1. Interests are an aspect of personality shaped by both hereditary and environmental factors.
2. Long-range, stable, occupational interests emerge during early teens, but mature interest patterns are not fixed for most individuals until an age of approximately twenty-five years.
3. Interests are not necessarily closely related to aptitudes or abilities.
4. Interests probably cannot be created *de novo* and in a short time merely by the classroom presentation of varied and vicarious experiences to youth. Such exposure may possibly, however, start the development of a new zone of interest, help fix existing interests, or uncover latent ones.
5. A strong motivation toward certain types of occupational or avocational behavior is expressed by a wide number of responses to an extremely wide range of stimuli.
6. Interests, as aspects of personality and as employed by the general clinical counselor, involve both acceptance and rejection of possible lines of activity. For example the typical worker with processes and things (mechanical interests) obtains interest scores which are negatively related to scores which measure a liking for persons and social situations.
7. The estimated, judged, or measured interests of secondary school and college students in an occupation seem to them to be and in fact often are quite unrelated to the training program they must take to prepare them for employment in the occupational family in which they have an identified dominant interest.
8. A legitimate interest in an occupational outlet often has little effect on grades earned in the curriculum leading to that outlet. Much of the training in a medical school may be largely quite unrelated to the particular aspects of medical practice toward which the interest is expressed.
9. Vocational and avocational interests appear to run in similar directions for a large proportion of individuals.
10. The interests of individuals tend to be less varied with increasing age.

Weingarten (1958) published a different kind of interest inventory called the *Picture Interest Inventory.* In responding to this inventory, the client reacts to triads of pictures rather than to words, phrases, or sentences.

Super and Crites (1962) have discussed various inventories used to measure vocational interests, with particular emphasis on the SVIB and the Kuder. They present in Table 29 (p. 382) the results of seven factor analyses of interest measures, but omit two important ones dealing with both the SVIB and the KPR-V: Cottle (1950a) and D'Arcy (1954). Super and Crites rename the factors pervading these various studies as scientific, social welfare, literary, material, systematic, and contact interests. Cottle and D'Arcy found similar factors pervading both the SVIB and Kuder. They describe them as liking for numerical-spatial activities versus linguistic activities, routine or business detail activities versus activities involving qualitative judgments, a masculinity versus femininity factor, contact with people versus scientific activities, aspiration for material evidence of success (money) versus productive evidence of success (products). It should be noted that, unlike the names proposed by Super and Crites, Cottle and D'Arcy each propose bipolar descriptions of interest factors.

Cottle and Downie (1960) devote a chapter to the topic of interests.

Tyler's (1964) chapter in Borow, *Man In A World At Work,* has one of the most recent summaries of current work using vocational interest inventories. She says:

> It has become possible to answer with increasing clarity theoretical questions about the structure of vocational interests. As we have already seen, Kuder found that there were clusters of interest items. Persons who preferred one of the activities in such a cluster were likely to prefer many of the others. Strong encountered evidence for relatedness when he correlated scores on the various occupational scales. Several factor-analytic studies using other items or tests have demonstrated that there are some main dimensions along which interests tend to arrange themselves. Persons who have worked on this research problem have come upon what seem to be many of the same major dimensions, regardless of the test or sample used. They differ somewhat, however, in the labels they attach to these dimensions. . . .
>
> For the practicing counselor, one of the most important generalizations to be drawn from several decades of research is that interest tests measure the *direction* rather than the *strength* of a person's interests. Because of the general meaning and connotation of the word 'interest,' a counselor who loses sight of this fact is likely to be puzzled by what looks like large discrepancies between interest and achievement. For instance, a college student gets an A on the Strong Author scale but fails his freshman composition course because he cannot bring himself to write themes. The A does not point to a compelling drive to get words on paper. It means only that he likes and dislikes the same sorts of things that writers like and dislike. Interpreting scores as answers to the question 'How much?' rather than 'What kind?' is probably the most common error in the use of interest tests. At present we have no technique except behavior observation for assessing how strong a person's drive is in the direction in which he wishes to go.

Holland (1966) has proposed one of the latest theories of interest development and vocational choice. His propositions are as follows:

Briefly, the theory consists of several simple ideas and their more complex elaborations. First, we assume that we can characterize people by their resemblance to one or more personality types. The closer a person's resemblance to a particular type, the more likely it is he will exhibit the personal traits and behaviors associated with that type. Second, we assume that the environments in which people live can be characterized by their resemblance to one or more model environments. Finally, we assume that the pairing of persons and environments leads to several outcomes that we can predict and understand from our knowledge of the personality types and the environmental models. These outcomes include vocational choice, vocational stability and achievement, personal stability, creative performance, and susceptibility to influence. . . .

In our culture, most persons can be categorized as one of six types — Realistic, Intellectual, Social, Conventional, Enterprising, and Artistic . . . . A 'type' is a model against which we can measure the real person. Each type is the product of a characteristic interaction between a particular heredity and a variety of cultural and personal forces, including peers, parents, other significant adults, social class, culture, and the physical environment. Out of his experience, a person develops habitual ways of coping with the tasks presented by his psychological, social and physical environment, including vocational situations. His biological and social heredity, coupled with his personal history, creates a characteristic set of abilities, perceptual skills and outlook, life goals, values, self-concepts (his image and evaluation of himself), and coping behavior (his typical methods of dealing with the problems of living). A type is then a complex cluster of personal attributes.

It can be seen from the foregoing that considerable thought, observation, and research has been devoted to the subject of vocational interest inventories over the last half century. Much of this has been made a matter of record, but there is still a considerable body of data resulting from empirical observations that is not in the literature and is thereby unknown to the counselor unless he happens to encounter persons who can tell it to him. Experienced persons in the profession should consider it an obligation to describe their experiences with these inventories so that new generations of counselors will be more effective with the instruments. Tentative hypotheses arising from such experiences can also be the focus of future research to test their value and expand the uses of the inventories.

The next chapter considers specific data about the inventories themselves.

4

Selected Vocational Interest, Preference, and Value Inventories

The material in this chapter focuses on the construction and interpretation of scores on the SVIB, the KPR-V, the MVII, the EPPS (Edwards Personal Preference Schedule), and the *Allport-Vernon-Lindzey Study of Values*. As discussed earlier, a knowledge of inventory construction gives some cues to use of the information it provides. If an inventory, such as the SVIB, contrasts a group of professional or managerial persons in general and members of a specific occupational group, this contrast becomes a part of the interpretation, along with response sets and other idiosyncrasies of the instrument which are a function of its construction.

Interpretation of an instrument also depends upon what publishers *and* users have found to be important. In the case of the KPR-V, this becomes a matter of knowing what is recommended in the manual and knowing that users have identified patterns of scores, such as the high Scientific and Social Service scores found with beginning medical students, or the high Persuasive, Literary and Social Service scores found in some groups of pre-law and journalism students. In this way, the counselor enhances his knowledge of the inventory and his ability to use it effectively.

The Strong Vocational Interest Blanks

Construction

Strong utilized earlier work of Cowdery in his 1927 construction of the SVIB. He revised the SVIB-M in 1938 and the T399 Form for males appeared in 1966. The SVIB-W was published in 1933 and a revised form in 1966 for research use. Each inventory except T399 consists of 400 items to which the client responds by marking *Like* (L), *Indifferent* (I), or *Dislike* (D). Each inventory consists of eight parts dealing with the following areas: Occupations, School Subjects, Amusements, Activities, Peculiarities of People, Forced Choice of Activities (selected from sets of ten), Comparison Between Pairs of Items, and Self-ratings of Present Abilities and Attributes. Approximately 260 of the 400 items are the same in inventories for male and female. Reference to Table 1 shows that the inventories have a reading level beyond Grade 12, with the instructions more difficult to read than the items themselves.

Strong points out in the manual (1959) that interests change considerably between the ages of 15 and 20, and recommends that the SVIB not be used widely with individuals below age 17. Interest scores of persons under 20 will usually increase somewhat with age. It is probably wise to restrict the use of the inventories to high school students who are bright, who have a pronounced, stated, and demonstrated interest in a given area, or to college students and adults in professional, managerial, and semi-professional occupations.

Eighty-two percent in each occupational criterion group score above a *T*-score of 40. It should be noted that this concept is the familiar one of the normal distribution of scores but is apt to be overlooked due to stress on the overlap of the lowest sixth of the criterion group with the contrasting professional and managerial group-in-general. This latter group was produced by combining all the other criterion groups except that particular occupation being scored. This point of contrast, or "point of reference" as Strong calls it, seems to produce the greatest differentiation of a given occupational group. It should be noted also that this is *not* a "men (or women)-in-general" group but a *professional* group.

Ninety-seven percent of the members of the occupational criterion group score above the middle of the shaded or chance score area shown on the profile. Thus, scores below this point bear little resemblance to those of persons in the occupation and are much more typical of the general professional group used as a point of reference. It can then be said that these two points, a *T*-score of 40 and the middle of the shaded area, are critical points in the interpretation of scores. The farther below these points the client's score falls, the more his responses resemble the professional group-in-general and the less they resemble persons in that occupation.

Strong preferred 250 to 500 persons in his normative criterion groups, but usually there were from 250 to 300 persons in the professional group with which the scales were constructed and another 250 or more on which it was validated. The persons in these criterion groups are described in his 1943 volume. Usually they ranged in age from 25 to 60, with a mean age of 41. For the scales constructed before 1940, the average annual salary of members of the given occupational groups was $2500 (which is equivalent to $8,000 to $10,000 currently) and only persons working three years or more in the occupation were included in the sample. As far as possible, Strong used members of the appropriate national professional association as his sample. For scales constructed since 1938, the reader should refer to appropriate research, such as that of Kriedt (1949), Schwebel (1951), Strong and Tucker (1952), and Olheiser (1962). Revisions of the inventory have been in process for some time, but only the one for the SVIB-M has been published in final form. The revision called T399 (1966 Manual), because it has only 399 items instead of 400, tends to update items rather than make drastic changes in the instrument. A revision of the SVIB-W is still in process. For a purely statistical evaluation of T399 by a stated "disbeliever" in such instruments who has never used it, see Rothney (1967). Most of the SVIB discussions which follow pertain to research and empirical evidence collected before the T399 appeared.

Until now the scoring has been quite complex with item weights for a given occupational group ranging from minus 4 to plus 4. This produces raw scores from minus 200 to plus 200. In earlier years, when much of the arithmetic was done by hand, the algebraic addition of scores caused frequent errors. Today machine-scoring and computers have eliminated many of these errors. It is still advantageous for the counselor to have a system of checks to determine whether the profiles he receives appear to be relatively free from error. This system of checks has been indicated in piecemeal fashion in preceding chapters, but will be discussed in more detail under the specific form of the inventory to which they pertain.

Earlier it was customary to look on separate cards for each occupation to convert the obtained raw scores into *T*-scores. For those who still use such a system, a revised profile, like that in Figure 1 which was developed at the University of Kansas, can save considerable time. The approximate raw scores at the intervals on the profile for each scale make it possible to profile directly from the raw scores. For most SVIB users, however, it is simpler to have the inventory scored by machine.

Interpretation

Whether the computer card or a regular profile is used, the counselor may wish to mark arrows along the top at a T-score of 40 and at a T-score of 10. The T-score of 40 emphasizes the point above which a client's score resembles those of five-sixths of the persons within a particular occupation and the T-score of 10 represents a point below which practically no one in the criterion group scores. The counselor may also wish to place a mark in the middle of the shaded area for those occupations which appear to be important for a given client. This mark gives an added point of differentiation because it indicates the point below which *only three persons* in every one hundred in that particular occupation obtained scores. In these ways, the counselor can make it easier for a client to inspect and to understand his scores on the SVIB profile.

Although the manual recommends use of the letter grades in the interpretation of the profile, it has been the experience of this writer that both counselors and clients can use standard scores more effectively than letter scores once the basic points of standard scores have been explained to the client. It is useful to have a copy of the normal distribution like that shown in Figure 2 in a plastic folder, handy for counselor and client reference. Use of standard scores permits use of the same basic reference points used in discussion of other inventories and tests. Standard scores have more useful properties than percentiles. In most instances they provide the same information if the counselor has learned the transition points, i.e., that the upper boundary of the average group or middle 68 percent is the 84th percentile or a T-score of 60 and the lower boundary of this group is the 16th percentile or a T-score of 40. The interpretation of the SVIB scores from an occupational group, as indicated above, really begins at a T-score of 40 (a letter score of B plus) which differentiates the top five-sixths of the given occupational group from all other professional groups and from the lowest one-sixth of the occupational group mixed among the scores secured by the professional-in-general reference groups.

Within the limits of the response set effects discussed in Chapter 3, interpretation of these scores focuses on high *and* low scores; that is, responses like men or women in a given occupation *or* quite unlike these men or women and more like professional men or women-in-general in the case of low scores ($T = 10$ or less). This latter score is really at a point four standard deviations below the mean of the

FIGURE 2

The normal curve and varied derived scores.

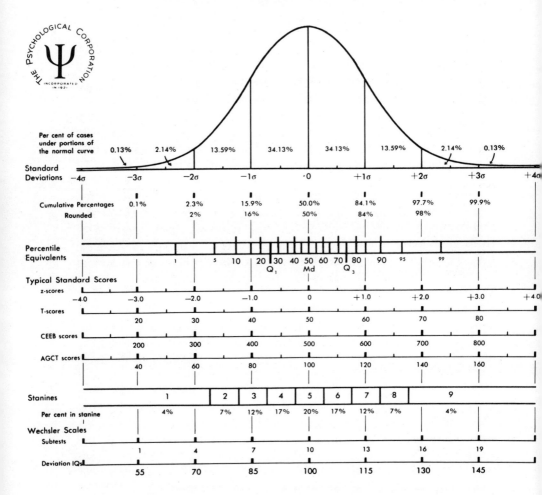

From Test Service Bulletin No. 48, The Psychological Corporation, 1955. Reprinted with permission.

criterion or occupational group or below the lowest one-tenth of one percent of this group. Thus a score below *T*-equals-10 is highly unlike that of members of the occupational criterion group.

As indicated in the discussion about checking for errors in the section on correlation coefficients of the SVIB and KPR-V in Chapter 3, the counselor learns to look for consistencies and inconsistencies within the instrument and with other sources of client data. In the case of the SVIB, some of these would be high scores on Group I and II scales and low scores on Group VIII and IX scales, or vice versa; high scores on Group V and the Interest Maturity Scale; the effect of high scores in Group IV occupations on lack of achievement in Engineering; the varying combinations of the non-occupational scores in relation to appropriate occupational scales, e.g., low masculinity scores on the SVIB-M and correspondingly high scores on Groups V and IX; high Occupational Level Scale scores and high scores on Groups IX and X; the proportion of responses scored Like, Indifferent, and Dislike to high and low scores on various occupational scales; and, a managerial pattern shown by a trend toward high scores on Production Manager, Personnel Manager, Public Administrator, Sales Manager, and President of a Manufacturing Concern. Some of these are substantiated by research; others are an outgrowth of observation but should still be a consideration of the counselor until research has clarified their meaning.

When considering relationships within any SVIB group of occupational scales, the counselor should remember that these represent an elementary form of factor analysis called cluster analysis. Any occupational scales correlating .60 or higher with each other are placed in the same group. In the case of the SVIB-M, these are shown in Figure 1. In the case of the SVIB-W, they are to be found in Strong (1943) and not considered outstanding or useful enough to be included in interpretation of the Women's Blank. (Only three groups were considered sufficiently related to be used: physical education teacher and nurse; social science teacher and YWCA secretary; and, artist, author, and librarian.)

It is obvious from the foregoing information that to interpret the SVIB, the counselor must have a considerable fund of information at his disposal. Not only must he know or sense relationships within the instrument, but he must know how to synthesize information within the instrument with data from sources outside the instrument, such as records and reports or information secured through interviews. Intensive study of findings of the various factor analytic research will also indicate how the counselor can identify various aspects of the linguistic-nonlinguistic patterns of interest and patterns of overall client behavior.

The Kuder Preference Record-Vocational

Construction

Kuder (1964) developed Form A of the *Preference Record-Vocational* using a pool of items administered to college students. He used a method of item analysis to construct scales whose items had high correlation with each other and low or moderate correlation with the items of other KPR-V scales. As shown in Table 4, this does not produce near-zero correlations but moderate correlations ranging from zero to .50. It does, however, operate to reduce the interrelations among the scales over those found in the intercorrelations among the scales of the SVIB. These are also shown in Table 4.

Kuder named these scales in terms of the nature of the items included in each one. Form A included Computational, Scientific, Persuasive, Artistic, Literary, Musical, and Social Service. Form B has the Mechanical Scale and Clerical Scale added and Form C has included the Outdoor Scale. Form E, intended for junior and senior high school use, has the same scales as Form C, but there are more items in each scale for higher reliability (N = 168) and the reading level of the items has been reduced to about sixth-grade level of difficulty.

The first type of item in Form A used a paired comparison process. This was changed in Form B to the triadic type of item used also in Form C and Form E. The respondent is asked to indicate which of the three choices he likes *most* and which he likes *least* in items like the following:

A. Repair automobiles and machinery,
B. Sell automobiles and machinery,
C. Write about automobiles and machinery.

Such a system permits six possible combinations of answers and provides much more coverage in less time than single items or pairs of items do. Reliabilities appear to be affected little by the difference in item form.

In Form C and Form E, Kuder added a validation scale called the Verification or V Scale. It is based on the assumption that if the respondent is unable to produce valid answers because he is careless, fails to understand the test, or gives ideal or socially desirable responses, his answers will resemble random answers. Kuder (1964) describes his verification scale as consisting of activities that "people in general, responding sincerely, tend *not* to select," even though the activities, for the most part, are socially desirable. Acceptable Verification Scores for Form C range from 38 to 44. Invalid scores fall below

38. The Verification Score for Form E is a score lower than 14, with the mean of chance scores at 24.67 ± 4.06.

Reliabilities are not as high as those reported for achievement tests. This is shown by test-retest correlations of Form E and Kuder-Richardson Formula 20 reliabilities for Form E (Kuder, 1964). They were computed separately for each sex and range from .70 to .94. The median test-retest coefficient for boys in Grade 6 is .81 and for Grade 7 is .86. Those for girls in Grade 6 is .87 and for Grade 7 is .86. Median Formula 20 reliabilities for boys in Grades 6–7 is .82 and for girls is .80. The reliabilities for senior high school students are somewhat higher.

The original Form D which is now used only when hand-scoring is desired has been replaced by the *Kuder Occupational Interest Survey* (KOIS), Form DD, which, unlike all of the other forms that deal with interest in *activities,* deals with interests compared to *occupational groups* similar to those of the SVIB. At this point, however, any similarity to the SVIB ends. The statistical construction, scoring, and interpretation in terms of occupational criterion groups and college major groups are considerably different. In constructing the KOIS-Form DD, Kuder (1966) used items dealing with seventeen areas of activity or interest. He took the ten original areas of the KPR-V, Form C, and added groups representing preference for: being active in groups; familiar and stable situations; working with ideas; avoiding conflict; directing or influencing others; working independently; and acting spontaneously in a carefree manner.

The KOIS, Form DD, covers 79 occupational scores and 20 college major scores for males and 56 occupational scores and 25 college major scores for females. Thirty-two scores for women are on scales developed for men. These scores derived from 100 triadic items are reported as lambda correlation coefficients derived by Clemans' method (1958), which is somewhat similar to a biserial correlation coefficient but which needs no assumption concerning shape of distribution of either variable. There are eight experimental scales, in addition to the 148 scales reported above, and a Verification Scale. The experimental scales are not ready for use, but contain possibilities for validation scales similar to those of the MMPI and for scales similar to the non-occupational scales of the SVIB-M. The Verification Scale scores between 45 and 60 indicate valid answers based on a sum derived from unit credits for specified responses.

The numerical scores describe the Clemans correlation reported as a series of X's beginning at .20, with each X equal to five correlation points. The score is also reported as a number for the same correlation. Almost all scores are positive and a factorial analysis is reported in the manual (Kuder, 1966).

The reading level is about sixth grade. The same reporting form is used for males and females. Intercorrelations of scales are low as a function of construction. Only seven are above .30 and none is above .40. The manual contains a description of the occupational groups.

Interpretation

With the exception of Form DD, which will be discussed separately, the profile for the KPR-V is based on appropriate normative groups from general population such as boys or girls in Grades 6–8 or 9–12, adult males or adult females. A percentile score is marked on each scale of the profile and standard scores are not available for these forms. Instead of the usual standard deviation units, Kuder uses quartile deviations and considers scores above the 75 percentile and below the 25 percentile as sufficiently different from the majority of persons in the normative group. The counselor is free, however, to use percentile scores of 84 and 16 as reference points of difference, if he wishes to make these scores comparable to scores of other inventories or cognitive tests he is using. The vertical percentile scale on each profile can also be used to illustrate how percentiles provide unequal units of dispersion; that is, how the distance between percentile scores increases from the middle of the distribution in either direction as scores approach the extremes of the distribution. For example, on the KPR-V profile for Form C, the distance between the 50th and 60th percentile is the same as that shown between the 98th and 99th percentile.

The interpretation of KOIS-Form DD scores is quite different. They are intended for use in helping potential school dropouts make occupational choices; with eleventh or twelfth graders in making educational or vocational choices; with college freshmen to select a major; or with adults for varied counseling purposes. The most useful way of grouping scores for an individual is to list in descending order the highest occupations and in another list, the highest college majors. There is no meaning attached to scores next to each other in such a list; that is, no relationship is inferred to adjoining scores.

The first point of reference for the counselor is the Verification Score shown in a box in the lower right corner of the counselor's copy of the report form. It should be at least 45 and no higher than 60. This is the first indication that the respondent has done the inventory candidly, has understood what he is doing, and has not tried to distort his responses. Another indication of lack of validity exists when an individual has no Clemans' correlational scores above .31 or if he has many scores between plus 10 and minus 10. Younger persons tend to have higher scores on scales representing college majors rather than on occupational scales while those for older persons are higher on the occupational scales. Kuder (1966) reports that about 80 percent of the members of thirty criterion groups studied obtained scale scores of .45 or more, with many above .60. High school students tend toward lower scores which are interpreted to mean less crystallized interests (lack of maturity of interest patterns).

In each of these report forms, it is the relative size of the scores that is most important. Occupational scores and college major scores should be considered separately. Inferences from the standard error of measurement (averaging about .02 for most scales) indicate that a difference of .07 between two scores represents a real or significant difference. Individual test-retest reliabilities for 92 high school senior boys ranged from .84 to .92. Thus occupations that fall within .06 of the top score in the occupational list or the college major list are considered significant scores with positive interpretation as long as they are above .31. Except for this, nothing is known about the meaning of low scores.

The first point of reference for the counselor using Form C and Form E is also the Verification Score. If it appears invalid, the counselor will have to decide what to do next. The usual procedure is to have the answer sheet rescored and also discuss with the client his approach to the test to see whether he felt he might have been careless or unable to read the items properly. If any of the conditions discussed earlier as typical of an invalid process appear, the counselor should *not* use that particular profile. Whether re-testing is advisable is the next decision to make.

The second step in interpretation is to note the high and low scores, using either the 75–25 percentile points or the 84–16 percentile points. Scores above and below these reference points either singly or in patterns show intratest relationships with other scales of the inventory, relationships with other data such as the corresponding scales and relationships with other inventories discussed in Chapter 3.

In addition to patterns mentioned previously, the counselor can look for patterns of high scores on Persuasive, Literary, and Social Service scales accompanied by low scores on Outdoor, Mechanical, Computational, and Scientific scales for individuals considering preparation for business contact occupations, law, or journalism. This is borne out in part by statistical studies quoted in Chapter 3 and by empirical observation. As the counselor uses the inventories and follows up clients to see what they have done, he gains further insight into information the inventory provides for the alert practitioner. It has been the experience of this writer over 25 years of using these inventories in counseling that the KPR-V scores and profiles remain relatively stable from Grade 9 on for the individual without serious personal problems. These scores tend to intensify as an individual progresses through school, but ordinarily do not change drastically unless the individual passes through some traumatic stage in his life with resultant drastic changes in behavior (Mallinson and Crumrine, 1952; Tutton, 1955). It should be noted here that in spite of the relationships with other data pointing toward occupational choice, the counselor using Form C or Form E at this time should talk to the client only about the kinds of interest in activities the scores represent, *not* their relationship to occupations, unless this latter relationship has been demonstrated by research. He can only make inferences about this to himself as points to be investigated on his later research or to be discussed with colleagues.

It has always seemed that to neglect the opportunity to treat a KPR-V Form B, C, or E profile as a series of ipsative scores is to miss an excellent opportunity to help a client gain insight into the interaction of forces these scores represent for him alone. If one were to compute the proportion of his score to the total score possible on each scale, this would permit treating these proportions as indicators of relative strength and weakness for him alone without reference to a normative group.

The Minnesota Vocational Interest Inventory

Construction

A new inventory which combines features of the SVIB and the KPR-V is the Minnesota Vocational Interest Inventory (Clark and Campbell, 1965). It is based on the differentiation of interest patterns of men in specific skilled and semi-skilled occupations from a reference group of "Tradesmen-in-General" (TIG). Responses given by the specific occupational group are scored as plus and those resembling the TIG group are scored as minus.

The inventory is composed of 158 triads in each of which the respondent chooses one response liked most *and* one liked least. Each triad contains three types of activities performed by skilled tradesmen. Thus the respondent chooses 316 responses and, although there is no time limit, the process requires less than 45 minutes. It is intended for use from ninth grade through adult levels and with students in college and technical schools intending employment in one of the occupations the inventory covers. Rothney (1967) has written a criticism of the MVII from the viewpoint of a statistician "nonuser."

Clark (1961) originally developed the MVII in an attempt begun in 1946 to differentiate the interests of men in various Navy ratings. At the present time, more than 7,000 civilian workers have contributed to the development of scales for twenty-one occupations. These occupations are listed below together with their percentages of overlap with the TIG group:

Baker (45%)
Carpenter (52%)
Electrician (31%)
Food Service Manager (39%)
Hospital Attendant (38%)
Industrial Arts Teacher (27%)
Machinist (41%)
Milk Wagon Driver
  (routeman) (43%)
Painter (42%)
Plasterer (37%)

Plumber (43%)
Pressman (32%)
Printer (37%)
Radio TV Repairman (27%)
Retail Sales Clerk (33%)
Sheet Metal Worker (49%)
Stock Clerk (63%)
Tabulating Machine Operator (30%)
Truck Driver (40%)
Truck Mechanic (57%)
Warehouseman (49%)

The process used to demonstrate the validity of these criterion groups versus the TIG group is Tilton's percentage of overlap. This represents approximately twice the percent of classification errors. The percentages of overlap for each Occupational Scale are indicated after each one in the list above. They range from 27% for Industrial Arts Teacher and Radio TV Repairman to 63% for Stock Clerk, with a median of 40%. This median is interpreted to mean that an overlap of 40% would misclassify 20 percent of the criterion group and the TIG group if the number in the group and the variances are approximately equal. Reliabilities of the Occupational Scales range from .64 to .88 with a median of .82. Those for the Area Scales range from .62 to .87 with a median of .83.

The MVII comes in two forms. One has separate booklets and answer sheets which can be hand-scored or machine-scored. Scoring stencils can be purchased for this form. The other form has the item booklet and answer sheet combined and can only be scored at a specified scoring service. In addition to the Occupational Scales, nine "Homogeneous or Area Scales" have been created from clusters of items highly correlated with each other. From inspection of the content items in each cluster and of the patterns of scores made on the Area Scales by the various Occupational Groups, the following names were given to the "Areas."

H-1 Mechanical
H-2 Health Service
H-3 Office Work
H-4 Electronics
H-5 Food Service

H-6 Carpentry
H-7 Sales-Office
H-8 Clean Hands
H-9 Outdoors

Research on these was conducted and described by Norman (1960).

Interpretation

As indicated, the MVII serves two purposes. The Occupational Scales show which group or groups the respondent's answers most or least resemble. The Area Scales show the patterns of the respondent's answers and describe for the counselor and client the interests characteristic of a given occupation in terms of the correlation between that Occupational Scale and a given Area Scale.

The Occupational Scales shown on the profile sheet are arranged in groups by means of cluster analysis provided by correlations among the scales. There are two major clusters: the first (3–7) contains Milk Wagon Driver, Retail Sales Clerk, Stock Clerk, Printer, and Tabulating Machine Operator; the second (15–19) is composed of Truck Mechanic, Industrial Arts Teacher, Sheet Metal Worker, Plumber, and Machinist. These two clusters are opposite poles of what appears to be the same factor. The other clusters are composed of Baker (1) and Food Service Manager (2); Carpenter (11), Painter (12), and Plasterer (13); and, Electrician (20) and Radio-TV Repairman (21).

The scores are reported as standard scores arranged so that two-thirds of any occupational group score above *T*-45 on that scale. The manual describes the critical scores used in interpretation by saying that persons with scores between 35 and 45 on an Occupational Scale are expressing fewer likes and dislikes similar to those of men in that occupation, those above 45 definitely share interests in common with men in that occupation, those with scores below 35 definitely have different interests from men in that occupation. The shaded area on each scale is an indication of scores like those made by the middle third of the TIG group on that scale. It is similar to that on the SVIB in that it reflects, through the amount of overlap, how easy it is to secure high scores on the scale. Scales with highest shaded area are Stock Clerk, Carpenter, and Truck Mechanic. Reference to the percent of overlap in the list of scales above shows that these three scales have the highest percent of overlap of the 21 Occupational Scales.

The highest and lowest Area Scale scores, containing items closely related to each other, describe for the counselor and the respondent the nature of the responses chosen. These make it possible to discuss the pattern of high and low scores in terms of interests characteristic of a given client. Each Area Scale is described by Clark and Campbell (1965) a little more elaborately than the Area Scale names themselves, but the scale names are representative of these descriptions.

Of all the more recent attempts to create new interest inventories the MVII seems to offer the most promise, both in terms of the research process by which it was developed and the type of clientele it is intended to serve. The MVII not only helps the respondent identify interest aspects of motivation, describing himself in relation to specific skilled and semi-skilled occupations, but it offers the first possibility of exploring the nature of these interests so that a counselor can help the noncollege-bound segment of the school population in occupational choice. It is unfortunate that at present the data relate to males, with only inferential use possible with females.

The Edwards Personal Preference Schedule

Construction

The *Personal Preference Schedule* was published by Edwards (1954, 1959) to provide an inventory of his version of fifteen psychological needs originally proposed by Murray (1938). He used Murray's names for the scales, but Edwards' description of these needs vary somewhat. Edwards had a secondary purpose in constructing this instrument: that of controlling for social desirability response set. The format of the inventory, using a forced choice of one item in each of 225 pairs of items, matched in terms of their social desirability according to the scaling method of successive intervals proposed by Edwards and Thurstone (1953), not only limited social desirability response set, but eliminated acquiescence response set found in "yes-no," "true-false" type items.

The inventory is untimed and takes from 40 to 50 minutes to complete. It can be machine-scored *or* hand-scored for the fifteen need scales, but the Consistency Scale can *only* be hand-scored. The consistency score is secured by comparing 15 sets of identical items on the answer sheet. Only half of these are included in the regular scoring of the other fifteen scales. The more sets that are answered alike, the higher the consistency score. Edwards (1959) says that a consistency score of 11 is at the .06 level of probability and, in his college normative sample of 749 females and 760 males, 75 percent of them scored at or above this point. He recommends, however, use of a score of 10 or higher which is scored by 87 percent in the college sample. Persons with consistency scores lower than 10 would have questionable scores on the fifteen *need* variables. Another check on the validity of a given answer sheet would be the number and nature of erasures and the items left unanswered on the blank. There is also a profile stability score computed by the correlation between the number of *A* responses in the 15 rows and the number of *B* responses in the 15 columns on the answer sheet. Edwards recommends a profile of stability coefficient of .44 (.05 level) as the point of significance. This was exceeded by 93 percent of the 299 cases on which it was computed, with an average correlation of .74.

When only a few items are left unanswered on the blank, these items are scored by tossing a coin and "heads" is marked *A*, "tails" marked *B* with a mark to show these items are chance responses. If many items are left unanswered, the blank should *not* be scored.

The college sample of 749 females and 760 males was combined and used to compute split-half reliability for each of the 15 need scales. These corrected reliabilities range from .60 for Deference to .87 for Heterosexuality, with a median of .78. Test-retest coefficients were computed on a group of 89 college students who retook the test within a one-week interval. These reliabilities ranged from .74 for Achievement and Exhibition to .88 for Abasement, with a median of .79. It should be noted that Edwards combined both sexes to produce these reliabilities and may have produced distortion, because in another place he says (1959):

> ". . . men have significantly higher means than women on Achievement, Autonomy, Dominance, Heterosexuality, and Aggression. Women, on the other hand, have significantly higher means than men on Deference, Affiliation, Intraception, Succorance, Abasement, Nurturance, and Change."

For these scales the overlapping distributions for males and females may have spuriously raised the reliabilities. (See pp. 85–86.)

The 15 variables show limited intercorrelation ranging from .01 for Affiliation and Intraception negatively and positively to .46 for Affiliation and Nurturance, computed on the college sample of 1509.

The only validity evidence is that between EPPS scores and self-rankings; other kinds of ratings are in correlation with the *Guilford-Martin Personnel Inventory*, the *Taylor Manifest Anxiety Scale* and the K Scale of the MMPI. None of these present very satisfactory evidence of validity, and it remains for research studies and empirical observations of counselors to provide the validity for the inventory.

In addition to normative data on the college sample, presented in percentile or *T*-score form, there are percentile norms for 4031 adult males and 4932 adult females described as "household heads who are members of a consumer purchase panel used for market surveys" (Edwards, 1959; Koponen, 1957).

Interpretation

The names of the fifteen scales of the EPPS and the meaning Edwards attaches to high scores on each scale are shown in Figure 3. They should be interpreted to clients in terms of the pattern of high *and* low scores, as well as in terms of the meaning of each scale given in Figure 3. For example, *high* scores on Achievement, Exhibition, Dominance, and Aggression along with *low* scores on Deference, Succorance, and Abasement have tended to cluster in a "leadership" pattern empirically observed in counseling. Another is the tendency for "proper young ladies" to get *high* scores on Affiliation, Succorance, Abasement, and Nurturance with *low* scores on Heterosexuality.

The counselor may find it useful to play down some of the names Edwards gave to these scales. For instance, instead of reference to Exhibition, he might say, "you would like (or "do not like," in the case of a low score) to be the life of the party" or "you would like to have people notice you more." Instead of reference to Heterosexuality, he might say, "You like mixed group activities" or, in case of a low score, "you don't seem very interested in mixed groups."

The counselor frequently notes that other client data are at variance with scale scores that might be expected to be related. For example, a client securing excellent marks in school may have an average or low Achievement score.

FIGURE 3
Edwards' Description of the EPPS variables (1959)

1. ach Achievement: To do one's best, to be successful, to accomplish tasks requiring skill and effort, to be a recognized authority, to accomplish something of great significance, to do a difficult job well, to solve difficult problems and puzzles, to be able to do things better than others, to write a great novel or play.

2. def Deference: To get suggestions from others, to find out what others think, to follow instructions and do what is expected, to praise others, to tell others that they have done a good job, to accept the leadership of others, to read about great men, to conform to custom and avoid the unconventional, to let others make decisions.

3. ord Order: To have written work neat and organized, to make plans before starting on a difficult task, to have things organized, to keep things neat and orderly, to make advance plans when taking a trip, to organize details of work, to keep letters and files according to some system, to have meals organized and a definite time for eating, to have things arranged so that they run smoothly without change.

4. exh Exhibition: To say witty and clever things, to tell amusing jokes and stories, to talk about personal adventures and experiences, to have others notice and comment upon one's appearance, to say things just to see what effect it will have on others, to talk about personal achievements, to be the center of attention, to use words that others do not know the meaning of, to ask questions others cannot answer.

5. aut Autonomy: To be able to come and go as desired, to say what one thinks about things, to be independent of others in making decisions, to feel free to do what one wants, to do things that are unconventional, to avoid situations where one is expected to conform, to do things without regard to what others may think, to criticize those in positions of authority, to avoid responsibilities and obligations.

6. aff Affiliation: To be loyal to friends, to participate in friendly groups, to do things for friends, to form new friendships, to make as many friends as possible, to share things with friends, to do things with friends rather than alone, to form strong attachments, to write letters to friends.

7. int Intraception: To analyze one's motives and feelings, to observe others, to understand how others feel about problems, to put one's self in another's place, to judge people by why they do things rather than by what they do, to analyze the behavior of others, to analyze the motives of others, to predict how others will act.

8. suc Succorance: To have others provide help when in trouble, to seek encouragement from others, to have others be kindly, to have others be sympathetic and understanding about personal problems, to receive a great deal of affection from others, to have others do favors cheerfully, to be helped by others when depressed, to have others feel sorry when one is sick, to have a fuss made over one when hurt.

9. dom Dominance: To argue for one's point of view, to be a leader in groups to which one belongs, to be regarded by others as a leader, to be elected or appointed chairman of committees, to make group decisions, to settle arguments and disputes between others, to persuade and influence others to do what one wants, to supervise and direct the actions of others, to tell others how to do their jobs.

10. aba Abasement: To feel guilty when one does something wrong, to accept blame when things do not go right, to feel that personal pain and misery suffered does more good than harm, to feel the need for punishment for wrong doing, to feel better when giving in and avoiding a fight than when having one's own way, to feel the need for confession of errors, to feel depressed by inability to handle situations, to feel timid in the presence of superiors, to feel inferior to others in most respects.

11. nur Nurturance: To help friends when they are in trouble, to assist others less fortunate, to treat others with kindness and sympathy, to forgive others, to do small favors for others, to be generous with others, to sympathize with others who are hurt or sick, to show a great deal of affection toward others, to have others confide in one about personal problems.

12. chg Change: To do new and different things, to travel, to meet new people, to experience novelty and change in daily routine, to experiment and try new things, to eat in new and different places, to try new and different jobs, to move about the country and live in different places, to participate in new fads and fashions.

13. end Endurance: To keep at a job until it is finished, to complete any job undertaken, to work hard at a task, to keep at a puzzle or problem until it is solved, to work at a single job before taking on others, to stay up late working in order to get a job done, to put in long hours of work without distraction, to stick at a problem even though it may seem as if no progress is being made, to avoid being interrupted while at work.

14. het Heterosexuality: To go out with members of the opposite sex, to engage in social activities with the opposite sex, to be in love with someone of the opposite sex, to kiss those of the opposite sex, to be regarded as physically attractive by those of the opposite sex, to participate in discussions about sex, to read books and plays involving sex, to listen to or to tell jokes involving sex, to become sexually excited.

15. agg Aggression: To attack contrary points of view, to tell others what one thinks about them, to criticize others publicly, to make fun of others, to tell others off when disagreeing with them, to get revenge for insults, to become angry, to blame others when things go wrong, to read newspaper accounts of violence.*

Investigation often shows that this aspect of behavior, accomplishment in school, may be such an accepted pattern for that client that it is *not* perceived as important among the 225 choices of the EPPS, and choices affecting some other scale are selected instead. It is not that this is unimportant, but that it is almost a conditioned behavior at a low level of awareness.

It would seem most advisable and consistent for the counselor to use *T*-scores in his interpretation with the same high and low cut points of 40 and 60 that he uses with other inventories. He talks to the client about the high scores indicating areas of most importance and the low scores indicating areas of least importance *at this time, among these 15 scores.* He also synthesizes these scores with the other client data available in making his interpretation, so that the client is helped to fit the data together before he makes decisions.

In addition to using scores from normative data, like the KPR-V, the EPPS lends itself to an ipsative interpretation because there is a possible score of 28 for each of the fifteen variables. This permits a counselor-client discussion of the meaning of these scores for that client, with no reference made to members of a normative group.

Use of adult male and female norms makes this inventory available for counseling hard-core unemployed or for the adult group that Hahn (1963, 1967) has described as the "mature, self-actualizing client." The reading level for the directions is sixth grade level and that for the test itself is seventh grade.

The Study of Values

Construction

The *Allport-Vernon-Lindzey Study of Values* (1951), as revised, attempts to determine relative strength of six basic areas of motivation

---

*Reproduced by permission. Copyright, 1954, 1959, The Psychological Corporation, New York, N.Y. All rights reserved.

for college students and adults. These areas are based on theoretical, economic, aesthetic, social, political, and religious values of Spranger's types and indicate the desired means to a goal or goals for a given individual. There are 120 scored responses with 20 possible for each of the six areas. The test is composed of 30 pairs of choices, rated as zero or three for each pair and 15 four-option multiple choice items rated by the respondent on a scale of 1 to 4. In these latter items, each option in the item is ranked 1, 2, 3, or 4 with no duplicating values within the item. This produces a ranking or forced choice within each item among four of the six values. The scores on each page are added and transferred to a score sheet. After a simple correction formula is applied, a profile of the scores is plotted.

The same administrative procedure is followed that has been discussed previously for inventories in general. Reliabilities for the revised (1951) form are given in Table 5, but no information about sex of the individuals in the samples is given, although the manual shows there are differences in sex norms.

TABLE 5

Reported Reliabilities for The Study of Values (1951)

Scale	Split-half N = 100	Test-retest (1 month) N = 34
Theoretical	.73	.87
Economic	.87	.92
Aesthetic	.80	.90
Social	.82	.77
Political	.77	.90
Religious	.90	.91

Evidence of validity is presented in terms of empirical observations of higher scores for women than for men on scales for religious, social and aesthetic values and higher scores for engineering students in theoretical and economic values. Expected differences in mean scores among six academic groups are shown by reported means on page 6 of the manual. They are for males in engineering, business administration, medicine, and graduate education courses as well as for clergymen and theological students (sex not indicated in the latter two).

The reading level of the test according to the Forbes formula (1953) is Grade 9.6 for the instructions and Grade 12.4 for the items. For more detailed information about reading level in terms of the major readability formulas, see Table 1.

Interpretation

In addition to the information given above pertaining to interpretation of scores as well as to the construction of the instrument, the manual presents a limited discussion of Spranger's types of men as the major basis for interpretation of a respondent's scores. It points out that the values of the theoretical man may be described as more objectively, rationally, and cognitively based. Economic values are utilitarian and practical, being primarily business values. Those for the aesthetic scale represent interest in art and beauty as found in daily life with a strong emphasis on the individual and his freedom. The values for the social scale center around service to and respect or love for people as the focus or purpose behind all behavior. This latter interpretation appears closely related to religious values also. The political man is interested in the power motive and manipulation of people as a direct basis for personal activities. Primary scores in the area of religious values, in addition to the obvious meaning, indicate the individual who seeks to attune himself to life in all its forms.

The counselor should bear in mind that no client presents a clear emphasis on only one of these values. As in the inventories discussed previously, the scores should be interpreted in terms of the pattern of high and low scores and the relationship of such pronounced values to other client data. For example, one would expect a client whose interests on the SVIB were highly similar to engineers and chemists and low in the business scales and whose measures of cognitive skills and achievement were higher in the nonlinguistic area, to secure high scores on the Theoretical Scale and low on the Aesthetic Scale, with possible high score on Economic or Political Scales and possible low scores in Religious and Social Scales in that order. Scores in these areas can also be treated as ipsative scores.

Conclusion

These descriptions of the construction and interpretation of the five instruments are necessarily brief and limited. The reader is referred to texts like Super and Crites (1962) for more detailed descriptions of research on each of the inventories and to the manual for each inventory for more details about the construction and standardization. The major focus in this chapter has been upon knowledge the counselor needs before he can begin to interpret the inventory to clients. If he has any professional interest, however, as he finds a given inventory to have a fruitful purpose for him and for his clients, he will assume the responsibility for expanding the data presented here to increase his own counseling effectiveness.

5

The Counselor's Approach
to Personality Inventories

Just as there is a general conceptual framework for the use of interest inventories (see Chapter 3), so there is a series of concepts which provide the framework for the use of structured personality inventories. The same general principles of administration, scoring, and interpretation that have been discussed previously for interest inventories apply; that is, the respondent should be advised to work as rapidly as possible, even though there is no time limit; he should be told a single item has little or no meaning by itself; scoring is usually done by machine with the request that answer sheets be returned; profiles are interpreted in terms of patterns of high *and* low scores and also in terms of comparison to an appropriate normative group; in some cases, ipsative scores could be developed but are apt to be less meaningful than for the inventories discussed in Chapter 4.

The scores from a structured personality inventory are considered to be a description of *how* an individual behaves, not *why* he does something. The *why* of behavior must still be discovered through other processes, such as interest and value inventories or interviews. Responses to a personality inventory comprise the client's attempt to describe for himself and for specific others, such as the counselor, how he sees himself in terms of the behavior described in each of the inventory items. To the extent that these items are clear and unambiguous descriptions of behavior, his responses do this. If the choices he is given fit him, he can describe himself effectively. To the extent that he is able to face himself or able to have others see him as he thinks he is, these item choices provide a picture of his behavior as he perceives himself. Whatever limits the above conditions place upon his perceptions they also place upon his ability to provide a description of himself congruent with his behavior as perceived by others. It is the counselor's job to create conditions which aid the respondent to do this in order to help produce data useful in self-understanding, self-acceptance, and behavior modification.

For this reason, the structuring that the counselor attempts prior to exposing a client to such an inventory can be of great importance in determining the reliability and validity of responses and of scores. The respondent should be told that the inventory is to be used to save time in building up a picture of his behavior as well as to offer a more objective means of checking on client and counselor perceptions of the client. He should be told that, because of machine-scoring and the manner the scores are to be used, no one is interested in or looks at his response to a given item; only the cumulative effect of items as reflected in his score for each scale and in the pattern of interactions among the scales of the total inventory is viewed. The counselor should discuss with him the concept that these scores show in an organized way how he sees himself and how he tends to interact with others, that such scores show how he differs from other people and how he describes his behavior as like or unlike that of other people. If the counselor feels the client can stand the idea, he may also point out that the scores can substantiate other data in indicating how serious any behavior problems may be and what type of professional help would appear to be most useful.

The most effective use of such an inventory occurs after the client understands its purpose for him and *willingly* undertakes completion. Not only must he grant permission for the results to be used in the manner the counselor describes to him, but other persons having authority over him should be asked to grant their permission as well. In the case of parents or guardian of a minor, the counselor should explain the purpose of the inventory as he and his client intend it and ask if the parents or guardian object to this. Agency policy and legal requirements should determine whether such permission is oral or in writing. Such contact with parents usually requires that an inventory be administered to one or a few individuals at a time. This permits more control over the circumstances of testing as well as making it easier to get permission to administer the inventory. The counselor should also remember to notify his administrator and secure his permission to give the inventory in case this is necessary for each administration. A sounder policy is to explain carefully the purpose of the inventory to the administrator and the circumstances under which it will be used. This should provide a general policy under which the counselor can use such an instrument without having to do more than notify the administration whenever he uses it. It is recommended that personality inventories be used sparingly and very carefully below the college level.

As in the case of the interest inventory, the personality inventory presents problems of reliability and validity different from those posed by cognitive tests. The individual responding changes with time so that it is impossible to secure a second administration of the instrument which is exactly equivalent to the first administration. This requires that reliability evidence be dependent on a single administration or successive administrations of the inventory over a short period which poses problems. A single administration necessitates either split-half or Kuder-Richardson reliabilities. Split-half reliabilities are useful only to the extent that successive items are comparable or homogeneous and measure approximately the same thing. In personality inventories, this is not apt to be the case, so such a method usually produces lower reliabilities than may actually exist. Split-half and Kuder-Richardson reliabilities are measures of internal consistency rather than stability and are less appropriate for measures of affect than for those measuring cognition. The use of test-retest reliabilities computed over a one-week interval may be distorted by the usual errors attributed to test-retest reliabilities, but more important in their use with personality inventories is the "mood versus character" nature of the various scales as discussed by Welsh (1952). He points out that some scales measure elements of behavior which vary from time to time and these are referred to as *mood* scales. Other scales tend to be relatively stable over longer periods, and these are called *character* scales. Obviously, the greater variability of the mood scales will affect reliability coefficients secured by test-retest methods. So also will traumatic experiences or changed set which occur between testings. As a consequence, it is difficult to secure reliabilities for personality inventories higher than .70 or .80 in contrast to those for measures of cognition which frequently reach .90.

The problems of reliabilities mentioned above set limits to the validities which can be demonstrated for personality inventories. The most common validities shown are based on content, concurrent, or construct validities. The first two of these are the most common with personality inventories, with *construct validity* occurring in the case of factorially developed inventories such as the GZTS which used factor analysis procedures to construct a new instrument from previously validated inventories. Most of the personality inventory items have evidenced *content validity* because they have been adapted from items used in psychological or psychiatric settings or items from previously validated inventories. An example of this would be the source of items for the MMPI or the CPI. *Concurrent validities* are those evidenced by an inventory like the MMPI which uses criterion groups and item analysis techniques in the construction of some of the scales. Tests of significance, demonstrating statistical differences between the criterion group and another group not possessing the given attribute of the criterion group, are used as evidence of concurrent validity.

Predictive validities, as shown by correlation of the scales of the inventory with other evidence of the behavior purportedly measured by the scale, are much more difficult to secure than for other types of tests. There are so many more errors inherent in the criterion measure and so much more variability and complexity of interaction in the behavior measured by personality inventories that predictive validities high enough to give clear evidence of validity are difficult to find.

Another complication in producing validities high enough to support use of personality inventories is created by the effect of response set upon the scores of inventory scales. One of the first articles attempting to identify response sets and their effect on scores of personality inventories was that of Cottle and Powell (1951) and one of the most recent is the monograph by Block (1965). The article by Cottle and Powell points out two aspects of the effect of response set upon MMPI scores. Figure 4 compares the mean responses of 400 adult males (Cottle, 1949) and the mean responses of 50 randomly-answered answer sheets of the MMPI. As would be expected, the means of the randomly-answered MMPI's were approximately half the possible number of responses for each scale and presented a profile of means in the abnormal range on all of the MMPI scales. This is in contrast to the means of the responses representing the 400 adult males in Figure 4 and the 179 Kansas University male students in Figure 5 which vary about a T-score of 50 on all scales of the MMPI. This is interpreted to mean that it takes the integrating effect of a human personality to produce scores on the MMPI within the normal range ($T = 30$ to $T = 70$). Conversely, scores produced by an individual in the "abnormal" range ($T = 70$ or more) on *selected* scales, while resembling random effects, by the very fact that these are selected scales and not *all* of the scales, is also evidence of the validity of the inventory profile for that person.

Cottle and Powell also marked one MMPI answer sheet all *True* and another all *False*. The results of this are shown in Figure 5 in contrast to the scores of 179 Kansas University male students. It is obvious from

FIGURE 4

T-scores of mean raw scores on the MMPI for 50 blanks answered by dice and random numbers; and for 400 adult college males at Syracuse University.

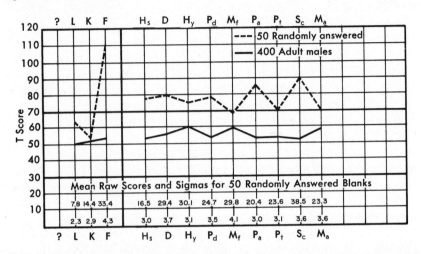

FIGURE 5

T-scores of raw scores on the MMPI for a blank answered all true and one answered all false, and T-scores of mean raw scores of 179 college males at the University of Kansas.

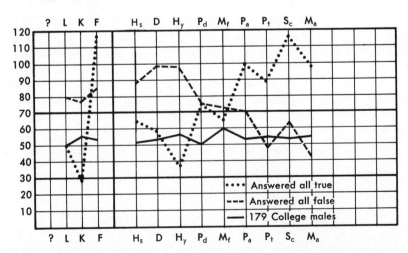

Figures 4 and 5 reprinted with permission from Cottle, W.C., and Powell, J.O., "The effect of random answers to the MMPI." *Educational and Psychological Measurement*, Vol. 11, 1951, p. 225.

these results that a preponderance of *true* responses produces a psychotic profile, while a preponderance of *false* responses produces increase in the scores of the neurotic scales. (*The total of true and of false responses found on the answer sheet of the MMPI should be reported on every profile sheet.*) This is interpreted as evidence that acquiescence response set is operating among the items of the MMPI and selectively influencing scores on the various MMPI scales. Whether this response set is an artifact of inventory items or is a personality attribute in itself is not clear at present. Because of this phenomenon, the professional person using results from personality inventories needs to modify his interpretation in the direction of caution until its meaning is clear.

Block (1965) has gone to considerable length to demonstrate that acquiescence and social desirability response sets do not destroy the usefulness of the MMPI. His monograph devotes itself to varying statistical processes by which he claims to determine this. However, his conclusion that "(1) acquiescent-response set is *not* a significant component underlying the MMPI and (2) the social desirability interpretation, although seemingly applicable in many MMPI contexts, has achieved its support for fortuitous and epiphenomenal reasons" is too broad a statement and needs much more qualification. He does throw considerable light on the limited effect these response sets have on MMPI scores, but they cannot just be brushed aside. They need to be recognized as an identified effect in the meaning of the inventory for the respondent, and this is still not clear. It is possible from Block's work to say what response set does *not* do in the MMPI, but it is still necessary to identify its real effect and meaning.

As Dahlstrom (1962) points out in discussing social desirability and acquiescence,

> The scales derived by searching for items which distinguish various clearly specified groups turn out to do a much better job in identifying and tracing changes in the operation of strong impression formation sets than do those scales developed by judgments alone . . . . What is needed for correct personality inferences is evidence that the scales have a single source of valid variance. . . . This kind of uniformity must be demonstrated by the usual procedures for establishing a scale's construct validity . . . . Such scales will probably always have to be used in combination with other measures specifically designed to check on various extraneous, undesired sources of response variance.

Other evidence of validity is contained in the intercorrelation between the scales of inventories like the MMPI and the CPI and between the scales of one inventory and those of another. In order to identify the sources of these relationships, factor analytic studies have been carried out.

Table 6 is one example of relationships within and between inventories. It describes the intercorrelations of the MMPI and those of the *Bell Adjustment Inventory* and the correlations between the two inventories. It will be remembered that Table 3 showed very low relationships between scales of personality and interest inventories, possibly because of the heterogeneous nature of the scales and the population sample. In Table 6, however, fairly sizable relationships appear between personality inventory scales which are not only significantly different from zero, but indicate considerable association with other scales. The MMPI F scale has correlations of .55 with Pt and .63 with Sc. The Hs scale correlates .51 with D, .59 with Hy, and .56 with Pt. This is the relationship usually referred to as the Neurotic Triad (Hs, D, Hy) and the accompanying rise in Pt as D rises. These scales are also the basic ones Welsh (1952) used to develop the Anxiety Index.

Moving beyond these relationships within the instrument, the correlation of .62 with the Health scale of the Bell offers support for the description of Hypochondriasis contained in the MMPI. In addition to the relationships within the Neurotic Triad above, Depression correlates .58 with Pt, which supports the contention that these two scales rising together reflect the amount of pressure the individual is under. The correlation of the Pt scale with the Sc scale of .84 reflects the relatively normal state of the population sample, because Hathaway and McKinley (1943) point out that as the population shifts from "normal" toward "abnormal" the correlation decreases (from .84 to .75). The Pt scale also shows a high correlation with the Sociability and Emotionality scales of the Bell, .52 and .78, respectively. This seems to support the hypothesis that the Pt scale and the Bell Emotionality scale contain items that measure related aspects of behavior. Inspection of the items in the two scales indicates these could be aspects of emotional condition and the correlations of .50 or higher between the Emotionality scale of the Bell and the other three scales of the Bell support such an hypothesis. In order to explore this hypothesis further, a factorial analysis would be necessary. Such an analysis by Cottle (1949) and by Wheeler and others (1951) throws some light on this area. Each of these studies identified a "neurotic" factor and a "psychotic" factor in the MMPI.

Successive factor analyses and item analyses have provided other factors depending upon the method chosen and the population sample available. A number of these have been discussed in Dahlstrom and Welsh (1960). The major point illustrated here is that correlations indicate a relationship among the behaviors measured by the various

TABLE 6

Intercorrelations of the MMPI and the Bell and Correlations Between the MMPI and the Bell

TEST		Minn. Multiphasic Personality Inventory											Bell Adj. Inv.			
		L	F	Hs	D	Hy	Pd	Mf	Pa	Pt	Sc	Ma	Ho	He	So	Em
		1	2	3	4	5	6	7	8	9	10	11	31	32	33	34
Minn. Multiphasic	L 1		-.16	-.14	.03	.14	.12	-.10	-.01	-.31	-.32	-.25	-.24	-.14	-.09	-.29
	F 2			.40	.34	.16	.45	.25	.21	.55	.63	.32	.37	.28	.25	.40
	Hs 3				.51	.59	.35	.22	.18	.56	.49	.28	.31	.62	.19	.43
	D 4					.42	.39	.28	.26	.58	.45	-.08	.21	.29	.40	.43
	Hy 5						.29	.18	.28	.18	.15	.04	.11	.40	-.07	.10
	Pd 6							.28	.33	.50	.54	.29	.47	.24	.18	.41
	Mf 7								.32	.38	.33	.04	.23	.18	.15	.35
	Pa 8									.36	.42	.11	.23	.14	.19	.33
	Pt 9										.84	.36	.49	.41	.52	.78
	Sc 10											.46	.52	.35	.44	.66
	Ma 11												.32	.25	-.05	.23
Bell	Ho 31													.33	.24	.51
	He 32														.18	.50
	So 33															.57
	Em 34															

scales. To shed light on the nature and meaning of these relationships, one must turn to factor analysis. The process and subjects chosen for such a factor analysis in turn limit the results that will be secured. The person who interprets such results will also illuminate or obscure the meaning involved. In the end, it is the interpreter who contributes the error and hence the confusion in meaning.

The professional person using structured personality inventories should bear in mind that the manner in which they are constructed, the conditions under which they are administered, the nature of the research conducted upon a given instrument, and the empirical evidence collected and published are all a part of the background of knowledge from which the counselor brings meaning to the scores of a given client. Such meaning must be tempered in turn by other client data available to the counselor which substantiate or raise questions about the validity of the scores being interpreted.

Used with caution and care, personality inventories can help a client grow in self-understanding.

The Development of Personality Inventories

During World War I Woodworth sought a method for testing groups of men to screen out those psychologically unfit for military duty. He used items adapted from psychiatric interviews and combined them in the *Personal Data Sheet*. This was the first structured personality inventory with forced-choice items in form similar to those in use today. Since that time many hundreds of inventories have been developed, but only the most frequently used will be mentioned here. Specific references dealing with each will not be listed because they can be found in Super (1949), Super and Crites (1962), Buros (1965), and Downie (1967).

Two inventories achieved widespread use in the 1930's: *The Bernreuter Personality Inventory* in 1933 and the *Bell Adjustment Inventories* published in 1934. A revised edition of the Bell appeared in 1962. The Bell has scales for home adjustment, health adjustment, social adjustment, and emotional adjustment. The Bernreuter scales cover neuroticism, introversion, dominance, self-confidence and solitariness. In a factor analysis of the Bernreuter by Flanagan, two factors emerged: neuroticism and self-sufficiency.

Another inventory published in 1934 intended for business and industrial use was the *Humm-Wadsworth Temperament Scale*. Permission to use this inventory is contingent upon a special training course given for a fee by the authors. The last of the inventories of the 1930's now in much use was the *California Test of Personality* available in forms extending from kindergarten through college and adult levels. This instrument was revised in 1952 and has been one of the few inventories available below the high school level. Although it has many subscales, the two major ones are total personal worth and total social adjustment.

The decade of the 1940's was the banner period for developing personality inventories. The *Mooney Problem Checklist* was published in 1941. This was not strictly an inventory. It presented from 7 to 11 problem areas according to the form of the test (junior high, senior high, or college), with subdivisions to be checked by the respondent and then explored by the counselor during the interviews. Another checklist published in 1949 was the *SRA Youth Inventory*. It provides places to check problems related to school, future, self, others, home, dating and sex, health, general, and basic difficulty. Neither of these follows the usual format of forced-choice yes-no or true-false responses. The *Minnesota Personality Scale,* now obsolescent, was also published in 1941. It was the first personality inventory developed by factor analysis.

In 1943 one of the most popular and most involved personality inventories appeared; this was the MMPI. It will be discussed in considerable detail in Chapter 6. In the same year, the original edition of the *Myers-Briggs Type Indicator* became available. As revised in 1962, it is intended to cover four dichotomous scales describing Jungian types: extraversion vs. introversion, sensation vs. intuition, thinking vs. feeling, and judgment vs. perception.

The *Kuder Preference Record-Personal* mentioned earlier was made available in 1948 and revised in 1960. It has scores for group activity, stable situations, working with ideas, avoiding conflict, directing others, and verification. It has never seemed to attain the usage achieved by the *KPR-V.* The greatest number of well-known inventories appeared in 1949, including the *SRA Youth Inventory,* mentioned above. One of these was the *Guilford-Zimmerman Temperament Survey* (GZTS). It will be discussed later as an example of a personality inventory developed by factor-analytic methods. Another was the *Heston Personality Inventory* which has scores for analytical thinking, sociability, emotional stability, confidence, personal relations, and home satisfaction. Another inventory in this year was the *Sixteen Personality Factor Questionnaire* (revised 1963) claimed to measure all the main dimensions of personality identified by factor analysis. It is composed of 187 items devoted to interests, preferences, and self-reports of behavior, with ten or more items devoted to each factor. There is a short form of 105 items. The last inventory published in 1949 was the *Thurstone Temperament Schedule* (revised in 1953). It provides scores for active, vigorous, impulsive, dominant, stable, sociable, and reflective aspects of behavior.

The only recent inventories which have had much acceptance are the *Minnesota Counseling Inventory*, 1953; the *Gordon Personal Profile*, 1953; and the *Gordon Personal Inventory*, 1956. The latter two inventories are intended to complement each other. The Profile covers ascendancy, responsibility, emotional stability, and sociability. The Personal Inventory covers cautiousness, original thinking, personal relations, and vigor.

The *Minnesota Counseling Inventory* was derived from elements of the MMPI and the *Minnesota Personality Scale*. It covers the following nine areas: family relationships, social relationships, emotional stability, conformity, adjustment to reality, mood, leadership, validity, and question score. It has 355 items and is intended for counseling high school students.

These inventories have been developed to identify and describe aspects of behavior for counseling and psychotherapeutic purposes. It has been difficult to provide adequate evidence of reliability for most of them and still more difficult to secure validity evidence. Probably the most typical of these instruments are: the MMPI, the personality inventory on which the greatest amount of research has been conducted; the *California Psychological Inventory* (CPI), which seems to offer through its construction and content excellent potential for college, and possibly high school counseling; and the GZTS, an inventory constructed by factor analytic methods. The construction and interpretation of these inventories will be discussed in detail in the next chapter.

6

Selected
Personality Inventories

Knowledge of the construction and interpretation of a personality inventory is essential for the counselor attempting to use it to assist a client. As indicated by the general discussion of personality inventories in Chapter 5, it is obviously impossible to discuss each of the instruments which have been developed in the last fifty years in this way. For this reason, three typical inventories have been selected for discussion. The first of these, the MMPI, has been chosen because it is the most widely used structured personality inventory in the world, with the most research of any such instrument. There are more than 100 research articles on it appearing per year at present. The second inventory, the CPI, was developed out of Gough's work with the MMPI, with the difference that it is intended for use with normal subjects and standardized in part by the use of an adjective checklist. The third instrument, the GZTS, was chosen because it was typical of inventories constructed by factor analysis processes and because it also typifies many of the characteristics of personality inventories which need to be brought to the attention of counselors using them.

The Minnesota Multiphasic Personality Inventory

Construction

Hathaway and McKinley (1943, 1951) developed the MMPI for use by physicians to identify patients needing referral for psychiatric treatment. The first form consisted of 504 items, each on a separate card. These cards were sorted by the respondent into sections of a box marked, *True, False,* and *Cannot Say,* respectively. The inventory was soon increased to 550 items and when the booklet form was developed sixteen items were repeated on the back of the answer sheet for ease in scoring. These 566 items were constructed from material in textbooks in abnormal psychology, questions from psychiatric interviews, and other similar sources.

Originally there were three validating scales: the Question or Cannot Say score (?), the Lie Scale (L), and the Validity Scale (F). Later the K Scale, a suppressor variable, was added. There were nine clinical scales constructed by using criterion groups as described in the sections on the SVIB. These scales were: Hypochondriasis (Hs), Depression (D), Hysteria (Hy), Psychopathic deviate (Pd), Masculinity-femininity (Mf), Paranoia (Pa), Psychasthenia (Pt), Schizophrenia (Sc), and Hypomania (Ma). Later a tenth scale, Social introversion (Si), developed by Drake (1946) was added. These clinical scales are often referred to by numbers 1 through 9 to zero, respectively.

Many other scales have been developed since the initial scales were published. These are discussed and their content listed in Dahlstrom and Welsh (1960). All of the scoring services provide scores and a profile for the four validating scales and the ten clinical scales. A new profile developed by National Computer Systems provides scores for eleven of the newer scales as shown in Figure 6. The new scales included are: Welsh's First Factor (A), Welsh's Second Factor (R), Barron's Ego Strength (Es), Hanvik's Low Back Pain (Lb), Williams' Caudality (Ca), Navran's Dependency (Dy), Gough, et al. Dominance (Do), Gough, et al. Responsibility (Re), Gough's Prejudice (Pr), Gough's Social Status (St), and Cuadra's Control (Cn). These have been described in Dahlstrom and Welsh (1960) and in Hathaway and Briggs (1957).

With the exception of the Validating Scales, the Mf scale, and the Si scale, all the other Clinical Scales and the newer scales were constructed by contrasting responses of a selected criterion group possessing a given attribute or symptom and a control group not identified with such a condition. Most of the attributes in the original Clinical

FIGURE 6

NCS-MMPI Profile

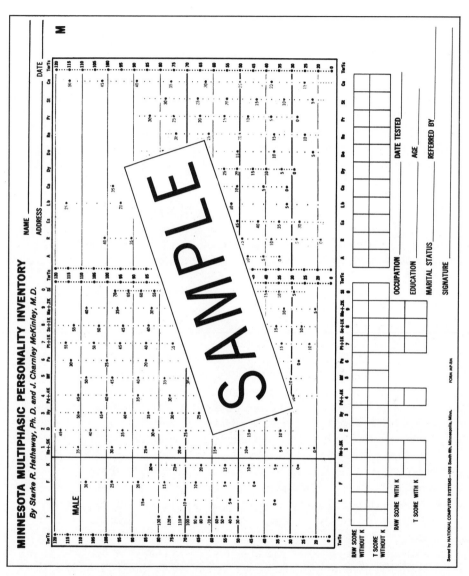

Adapted from the manual of the MMPI by permission. Published by The Psychological Corporation, Copyright 1943, 1951, The University of Minnesota Press. All rights reserved. Produced by National Computer Systems, Minneapolis, Minnesota.

Scales were psychiatric in nature and identified with the syndrome described by the scale, except for the Mf and Si Scales. The Mf Scale was constructed by selecting items that separated the sexes and others that characterized sex inverts. The Si Scale was constructed by selecting items that identified college women who were social introverts versus those who were social extroverts. Further statistical tests showed few sex differences, so the scale is used with both sexes.

A number of persons have proposed a coding system for filing and interpreting MMPI profiles. Notable among these have been Hathaway (1947), Welsh (1948, 1951) and Drake and Oetting (1959). The counselor in a school setting will have to decide how useful these are to him and then learn to use them through the preceding references and through Hathaway and Meehl (1951).

The Validating Scales were constructed somewhat differently. The fifteen Lie Scale items were selected because they represented choices opposite from those chosen by most people (not socially acceptable or popular). High scores on the Validity Scale (F) items indicated that the respondent was confused, careless, did not understand how he should answer the inventory, or that an error was made in scoring. Later research imputes other meanings to the F Scale which will be discussed further below and in the next section. The K Scale or Correction Factor was originally developed as a suppressor variable; that is, its use tended to heighten the predictive or descriptive value of several of the Clinical Scales. It was not possible to utilize both poles of this variable. A low score indicated a person who was overly self-critical and a high score described a person who was defensive and tried to cover up in his responses. Because the latter was considered the more serious psychological behavior, its effect was controlled for in the scoring of the test. As shown by the 1951 manual, fractions of the K score are added to Hs (.5), Pd (.4), Pt (1.0), Sc (1.0), and Ma (.2) to bring these scores up to what they presumably would have been if the respondent had been able to answer candidly. All three Validating Scales have been shown in varied combinations to indicate response sets under which the answers were given; that is, an L plus K score averaging more than a T-score of 67 identifies a respondent who tried to appear more normal (lower scores) than he really was (Cofer, et al., 1949).

With the exceptions noted above, according to the 1943 manual, the original Clinical Scales were constructed by contrasting the responses of persons not under psychiatric care with those of individuals psychiatrically diagnosed as having a particular syndrome of abnormal behavior. The criterion group for the Hs Scale was persons who were "unduly worried over their health" with physiological complaints for which there was no obvious basis. The Depression Scale used subjects diagnosed as being in the depressed phase of a manic-depressive psychosis described as "poor morale of the emotional type with a feeling of uselessness and inability to assume a normal optimism with regard to the future."

The 1943 manual describes the group from which the Hy Scale was derived as patients with conversion hysteria symptoms with general or specific physiological complaints. The criterion group for the Pd Scale was persons with psychopathic or character disorders rendering them incapable of deep emotional response, unable to profit from experience or who disregarded social mores. The Pa Scale items described individuals who were suspicious, overly sensitive, or had delusions of persecution. The criterion group for the Pt Scale were characterized by phobias or compulsive behavior. The differentiating items on the Sc Scale described "patients who are characterized by bizarre and unusual thoughts or behavior." Those for the Ma Scale described "persons with marked overproductivity in thought and action."

The general problems of computing reliabilities of personality inventories discussed in Chapter 5 apply to attempts to determine reliabilities of the scales of the MMPI. Three sets of test and retest reliabilities are presented in the 1951 manual: those by Hathaway and McKinley are only for six of the Clinical Scales, ranging from .57 to .83 with a median of .76; those by Holzberg and Alessi are based on 30 psychiatric patients on the Card Form without the K Scale and range from .52 to .93 with a median of .77 for the twelve scales reported; those by Cottle (1950b) are shown in Table 7. They are based on 32 females

TABLE 7

Correlation Coefficients and Related Estimates for Card vs. Booklet Form of the MMPI with 100 College Students

	N	L	K	F	Hs	D	Hy	Pd	Mf	Pa	Pt	Sc	Ma
r_{cb} Males	68	.51	.79	.77	.72	.65	.65	.81	.83	.53	.92	.90	.78
r_{cb} Females	32	.34	.72	.72	.91	.69	.83	.79	.79	.63	.87	.82	.75
r_{cb} (Product Moment)	100	.46	.76	.75	.81	.66	.72	.80	.91	.56	.90	.86	.76

and 68 males taking the Card and Booklet forms within a one-week period. The range of reliabilities for all scales except Cannot Say, which was not done, was from .46 (L) to .91 (Mf) with a median of .76.

One note of warning is indicated in Table 7. The Mf Scale for males is .83, while that for females is .79. However, the total correlation for the combined group of 100 males and females is .91. None of the other nine scales in Table 7 with a greater difference between males and females than the Mf Scale show a higher coefficient for the combined group of 100. It would appear that the .91 correlation for the combined group on Mf is a function of two overlapping distributions produced by combining scores of males and females on this variable. This seems to be one more instance where combining scores of both sexes on a variable is inappropriate.

Other than this qualification, the reported reliabilities appear to be about the size one secures from such inventories. Rosen (1966) has presented reliabilities for most of the newer scales described in Dahlstrom and Welsh (1960).

In addition to the validity evidenced in the construction of the scales using psychiatrically diagnosed groups (Hs or Hy) or contrasting groups (Mf and Si) as a criterion, research has shown other validities for most of the scales either singly or in combination. For example, the research of Cofer, et al., cited above provides validity for L plus K in combination. These studies will be cited under the section on Interpretation.

Factor analyses of the MMPI have also offered evidence of validity. These are cited in detail in Dahlstrom and Welsh (1960) and only selected ones will be commented upon here. Although there is some disagreement over the nature and names given the factors, a number of studies have found two group factors contributing to most of the variance within the MMPI (Cottle, 1950b; Wheeler, et al., 1951; and Welsh, 1956). Comrey has been attracted to factor analysis of each scale. While this sheds light on effect of the items, it has always seemed of limited value unless one were to construct new scales. As long as the present scales are to be used to classify respondents as like or unlike members of the criterion group *and the present items are able to do this,* the nature of these items is immaterial. As Dahlstrom and Welsh (1960) have pointed out, ". . . it has been found that scales like the ones in the MMPI work best against complex criteria when they contain items that have a high correlation with the criterion measure and *low* correlations with one another. Such items then are each bringing to the total scale quite independent but valid variance contributions." Identification or classification was the intended task of the inventory. It has proven to be too involved for use by physicians, or for that matter, by psychological technicians, psychological counselors, or counseling psychologists without considerable training under as much direct supervision as is usually given to mastery of projective instruments. The reading level of the MMPI as shown in Table 1 is grade 6.5 for the items and 7.3 for instructions.

Interpretation

There are three aspects in interpreting an MMPI profile to a respondent. One involves estimates of the set with which the respondent approached the inventory and is indicated by the various Validating Scales. Another is the interaction of the regular ten Clinical Scales. Still a third is the meaning the eleven newer scales contribute to a description of behavioral tendencies of a given client.

There are counselors who are quite concerned over how much they should tell a client about his MMPI scores. Actually the client only knows what the counselor tells him about this instrument, so it is permissible to show him the profile and interpret to him as much of it as the counselor estimates he can use effectively. As with other inventory profiles, the counselor usually uses a T-score of 40 and a T-score of 60 as marking the boundaries of the average group. He points out that unless client scores exceed these points, the scores are like those of most persons taking the instrument and they do not show how the client differs from most people. There are only three scores at present which have meaning in terms of T-scores below 40: the K Scale, Mf, and Si. So most of the meaning is discussed in terms of T-scores beyond 60. For persons in the normal range of behavior, this means patterns of T-scores between 60 and 70, and an occasional score above 70. For persons requiring psychotherapy, the inventory is discussed cautiously in terms of patterns of scores above a T-score of 70.

The needs of the usual counseling situation for which this monograph is intended dictate that interpretations discussed here be those for the 60–70 T-score group. Here the intent is to discuss tendencies in behavior with a client, using terms like: "Persons with scores like this usually . . . ," or, "This score describes a person who is . . . ," or "Your score seems to be telling us that. . . ."

In discussing the Validating Scales, the approach will be to describe meanings built into the construction of the instrument as modified by usage and research.

The Question or Cannot Say score shows the number of items left blank or unanswered. In the original card form of the MMPI which was intended for use primarily in a clinical setting, the very nature of that setting caused a score on this scale which is not found with the booklet form in common use today. The use of a box into which the patient placed the item cards in either True, False, or Cannot Say sections created a situation which encouraged respondents to put cards into the Cannot Say section. Using the inventory with disturbed patients also tended to increase the Question score with the Card form because these respondents often find it more difficult to make the True or False choices required by the inventory. For these reasons, the older manual recommended that profiles with Question scores of more than 50 items be considered of questionable validity. Fortunately with the more general use of the Booklet form the conditioning of persons produced by cognitive testing to respond to *all* items has practically eliminated scores in the Cannot Say or Question category.

The 15-item Lie score was intended to identify persons with a tendency to mark items in a socially acceptable, but opposite fashion to that of most persons taking the MMPI. It has tended to identify respondents whose values are different from those of the normative group, but who are sincere in these responses, as well as identifying individuals who are trying to make themselves look more normal than they really are. As mentioned above, an L plus K *T*-score average greater than 67 characterized the respondent trying to secure a normal score or to *fake good*.

Originally, the 64-item F score was intended as an indicator of how well a respondent understood the instructions, how carefully he did the test, or whether errors had been made in scoring. Usage added evidence for the interpretation that a high F accompanied by high Pd tends to reflect family conflict and high F and high Sc may be indicating a tendency toward bizarre or odd response choices. Gough (1950) has shown that an F minus K index greater than a raw score of plus 9 identifies the intentional malingerer or respondent trying to *fake bad*.

The 30-item K score as discussed in the construction section was originally a statistical scale adding to the discrimination of Hs, Pd, Pt, Sc, and Ma by correcting those scores back to where they would be presumed to be, if the respondent had not been so defensive. It can also be interpreted in terms of a low score showing the individual who is overly self-critical or who makes himself look worse than he really is. This can be a neurotic function, or perhaps just a very candid response because he trusts his counselor, depending upon how low the score is. Recent research has indicated that K scores between *T*-equals-55 to 65 may reflect the "normal" demand for privacy of the individual who is saying, "Some of these questions are none of your business." Items of the K Scale have been used also in the initial development of *Edwards' Social Desirability Scale* and the *Taylor Manifest Anxiety Scale* (Dahlstrom and Welsh, 1960).

Singly and in patterns, the regular Clinical Scales help indicate various syndromes of exaggerated normal behavior and those of abnormal behavior. In the former case, they are indicating tendencies within the normal range and what might happen if the individual is put under the sort of pressures that destroy the balance among those elements within him that produce controlled, acceptable performance in life. Guthrie (1950) and Schmidt (1945) did some of the original work on identifying abnormal patterns of scores on the MMPI, and Hathaway and Meehl (1951) have presented extensive documentation of patterns and related case data. These deserve to be studied until the counselor begins to get the "feel" of the profiles and then should be used as a reference. The three basic patterns center around the Neurotic Triad (Hs, D, and Hy), the Psychotic Triad (Pa, Pt, and Sc), and combinations of Pd with F, Pa, and Ma.

In both the Neurotic and Psychotic Triads, a pattern with D or Pt as the high point indicates a better prognosis for counseling or psychotherapy because it is saying the individual is under pressure to make him more desirous of changing his behavior. This is reflected also in Welsh's (1952) Anxiety Index:

$$AI = \left[\frac{Hs + D + Hy}{3}\right] + [(D + PT) - (Hs + Hy)]$$

The farther the Anxiety Index moves above 50, the more it reflects increasing amounts of clinical anxiety. Dahlstrom and Welsh (1960), however, report that Welsh's first factor, the A scale, when used with the R scale, is a clearer indicator of anxiety. A pattern on these triads with D or Pt at the lowest part of a V shows a poorer prognosis for treatment because it indicates an individual who has developed pronounced enough defense mechanisms to make it difficult for him to change his behavior. This is also indicated by Welsh's (1952) Internalization Ratio:

$$IR = \frac{Hs + D + Pt}{Hy + Pd + Ma}$$

The more the IR departs from 1.00 in either direction, the more difficult it is to help a client modify or change behavior. A score below 1.00 indicates lack of control and direct expression of emotional difficulties, with a score above 1.00 reflecting internalizing problems with somatic symptoms and self-punishment. The R scale is supposed to be a more refined measure of this, but correlations of only .31 and .52 are reported with IR.

As far as the individual Clinical Scales are concerned, interpretation is focused about the description of the criterion group in the manual, tempered by observation and research. They are reported with abbreviations for the scale and the code number of the scale.

The 48-item *Hypochondriasis Scale* (Hs or 1) reflects a generalized overconcern about health. This is more pronounced than that of the average person and is not as often accompanied by systemic complaints as in Hy. It is found also in persons with physical handicaps and disabilities, but observation of these persons seems to indicate that as they are able to accept their limitation more completely, the Hs score decreases. The question is frequently raised about the meaning of items on Hs and Hy such as, "Do you have *frequent* colds?" Questions focus on how to interpret the word "frequent." Does it mean every month, every six months, or what? Observations from use of the MMPI seem to indicate that interpretation does not depend on meaning of a single item, but rather on the cumulative impact of a series of items dealing with reaction to health or any other aspect of an individual's behavior. Hs tends to rise with Hy in all profiles except the psychotic patterns where it tends to be higher, with Hy the lowest in the Neurotic Triad. The use of Hs by itself has questionable value in psychological counseling. Its interpretation takes on more validity and meaning in terms of its position in the pattern of scores on the whole MMPI profile. There are 20 of the same items on the Hs and Hy scales, so there is bound to be overlap and correlation between the two scales.

The 60-item *Depression Scale* (D or 2) indicates the amount of psychological pressure a person is under with concomitant feelings of poor morale and pessimism. The criterion group on whom the scale was developed represented 50 fairly pure cases of depression with the bulk of cases in the depressed phase of manic-depressive psychosis. The normative group was married persons not under treatment, college students, and some normals with high scores on the preliminary D scale.

When discussing a rise in the D score with a client in a counseling interview, the counselor might say, "A score like this ($T = 60-70$) indicates that you were under a fair amount of pressure when you did the inventory. It describes a person who is moody and blue and who seems to lack hope about the future."

As discussed above, when the items of the D Scale produce a score which is the high point of the Neurotic Triad, the respondent is indicating more readiness for counseling and more willingness to change his behavior. However, with sharp rises in D and Pt above a *T*-score of 70, Simon and Hales (1949) found evidence of a pre-suicidal pattern. When the D Scale is the lowest point in the Neurotic Triad, a pattern of temporary nonadjustive mechanisms is usually present so that the client takes refuge in psychosomatic behavior rather than actually changing his behavior to achieve a given goal.

The D score is the most frequent high score with abnormals and tends to appear in most of the patterns of scores on the MMPI, but it is of limited use in diagnosis when used alone. Used in combination with other scales, it has a variety of meanings. These are described in considerable detail in Dahlstrom and Welsh (1960). Most of their interpretations deal with application to varying populations of abnormals and will not be discussed here. The counselor who finds a high D score in combination with one or more other scales with normals should refer to Dahlstrom and Welsh for more detailed information.

The 60-item *Hysteria Scale* (Hy or 3) was originally described as showing the degree the respondent resembles patients with conversion hysteria symptoms as represented by various systemic complaints, such as headaches, stomach or intestinal upsets, or by more specific physical complaints. These items have a marked relationship to education and to age. College students average approximately one-half standard deviation above the normative group. Clinical observation leads to the hypothesis that high scores in the normal individual reflect a tendency to over-anticipate situations and to "clutch" under pressure so that performance is reduced. The combination of items confuses more precise interpretation of this scale except in combination with other scores as discussed previously.

The 50-item *Psychopathic Deviate Scale* (Pd or 4) was developed to identify the respondent who lacked ability to feel deeply, to assume responsibility, or to abide by social mores. It was intended to indicate persons with character disorders, such as sex deviates, alcoholics, or criminals. Most of the criterion group were young male and female delinquents identified with minor, rather than capital offenses, and who had been remanded by the courts for psychiatric study. High scores within the normal range (60–70) seem to describe the person who dislikes rules and regulations or having to conform. This could be the very bright "normal" individual for whom many rules and regulations designed for the "average person" seem ridiculous or inappropriate; it could be a girl who wishes to carry on activities sanctioned only for boys in our society; it could be an individual with family conflicts; or it could be a delinquent who does not conform to society's rules. The interpretation has to be made in terms of the pattern of MMPI scores and their synthesis with other case data.

For example, the Pd Scale high with F often indicates family conflict; in combination with a high Ma score, it describes behavior frequently found in scholarship candidates and also in delinquents, here other information is necessary to show into which group the client should be classified; in combination with the scales of the Neurotic Triad, the Pd Scale may be reflecting behavior, such as alcoholism, produced in response to neurotic pressures. Obviously considerable experience with the scale and with synthesis of all case data are necessary before adequate and valid interpretation to a client is possible.

The 60-item *Masculinity-femininity* Scale (Mf or 5) was constructed by contrasting responses of males and females. Originally, the purpose was to identify homosexuals, but it was discovered they could conceal this behavior in responding to the items. The scale is more useful at present to identify a pattern of client behavior reflecting interests, attitudes, and values more like those of the opposite sex; that is, high scores for males *may* indicate homosexuality, but such scores are *more* apt to reflect an interest in people and communication activities (femininity) involving a fair degree of *linguistic* skills. High scores for females show motivations and behavior focusing upon non-word symbols such as those used in the sciences, an interest in scientific and mechanical processes and a liking for physical activities such as participating sports (masculinity) that can be described as *nonlinguistic* behavior. These italicized terms are more useful in discussing such scores with clients. Low scores are interpreted for each sex in terms of behavior described above that is characteristic for that sex *in the United States;* that is, the items were chosen to reflect abnormality, so the scores are interpreted opposite from those found on inventories like the SVIB or GZTS and show negative correlation with such scales of other inventories as noted in Chapter 3, Table 3.

College males tend to score higher than general population on the Mf Scale, with those interested in the humanities and social sciences scoring higher than those interested in the sciences, but all male college groups tending to score *above* the mean of general population. This behavior indication is a linguistic one and is also characteristic of college females, but their scores showing this are *below* the mean.

The 40-item *Paranoia Scale* (Pa or 6) describes behavior characteristic of an abnormal population who are suspicious, overly sensitive, and inclined toward delusions of persecution. In the 60–70 T-score range, it identifies persons who are socially inept and who tend to over-interpret the statements or actions of others. They are ill at ease in group settings, need help in developing social skills and in becoming more effective in their interpersonal relations. The behavior described by this scale is often associated with feeling of inferiority or low personal worth. It is frequently found in combination with Pd and Ma, particularly with female delinquents. The Pa Scale is seldom high by itself, but appears in varying combinations of normal and abnormal behavior. Typical examples of Pa Scale items for different codes are given in Dahlstrom and Welsh (1960). The Pa Scale high with Sc usually indicates behavior that is more difficult to change through counseling than that shown when the Psychotic Triad peaks at Pt.

The 48-item Psychasthenia Scale (Pt or 7) used as a criterion group patients with phobias or compulsive behavior with the items later subjected to an internal consistency item analysis. A score between T-60 and T-70 describes a person who is moderately compulsive and rigid, preferring to complete a task before leaving it, and preferring repetitive activities in the same pattern time after time. This type of person often seems to substitute worrying in place of an actual attack on the problem about which he is concerned or distracts himself with guilt feelings, has difficulty in concentrating, procrastinates in making decisions, and expresses feelings of low personal worth. As indicated earlier, the Pt Scale is most frequently high with D as an indication of the individual's response to psychological pressures and general maladjustive behavior. When it is the highest score in the Psychotic Triad along with elevated D score, it frequently shows a client who responds rapidly to counseling or psychotherapy, even though he is under considerable pressure and needs careful attention. The use of the Pt Scale as an indicator of "mood" along with Hs and D in the numerator of Welsh's (1952) Internalization Ratio is a point to be noted when considering reasons for fluctuation in this score.

The 78-item *Schizophrenia Scale* (Sc or 8) is the last of several attempts to produce a scale which would successfully separate schizophrenic patients from normal individuals. It has limited use by itself in the identification and description of schizophrenics. While its item content deals with bizarre or unusual behavior departing from that of the average person in the direction of disorientation or considerable day-dreaming, it is useful with *T*-scores of 60–70 to indicate an individual whose interests and behavior center about activities of a solitary nature, such as reading, hiking, hunting, fishing, or shop work, which do not necessarily indicate withdrawal, but often a healthy balance between activities requiring participation with people and those which do not. It should be noted that intercorrelations with Pt discussed above are higher with normals than with abnormals. Harris and Lingoes (1955) found that items separated into groups describe behavior which is different socially and emotionally, which shows lack of self-control in matters of an intellectual and emotional nature, and which reflects sensorimotor disfunction. There is considerable tendency for this scale to appear in combination with F, with Pa, or with Pt. The reader should refer to Dahlstrom and Welsh (1960) for more involved discussion of these patterns than is possible here.

The 46-item *Hypomania Scale* (Ma or 9) is supposed to reflect a lesser state of manic behavior than usually found with abnormals in a manic-depressive cycle. It is characterized by marked overproductivity of thought or action frequently never carried through to effective completion. There is considerable overlap between the behavior described by items of the Ma Scale and those of the Pd Scale. Often persons with character disorders are identified by scores on both scales. However, as indicated in the discussion of the Pd Scale, this seems to be characteristic of bright students as well, and any interpretation has to be made in light of data other than the scores above.

A score between 60 and 70 on the Ma Scale accompanied by a similar rise on the Pt Scale may reflect an individual who is quite uncomfortable because he undertakes too many tasks and his obsessive-compulsive tendencies force him to complete them. A rise on the Ma Scale accompanied by a correspondingly lowered D Scale, or vice versa, may indicate a minor manic-depressive cycle frequently observed with adolescent females, particularly college students. The position of Ma as a "character" scale denominator in Welsh's (1952) Internalization Ratio, along with Hy and Pd, should be noted as an indication of the difficulty in producing changes in the behavior shown by these items.

The 70-item *Social Introversion Scale* (Si or 0) is the last of the Clinical Scales and was added as a result of research by Drake (1946) with college women. Later studies showed the same phenomenon operating for college males, so interpretation of the scale was generalized to both sexes. A high score typifies the individual who prefers to limit his activities to those he can carry on alone or with a few people he knows quite well. While it is not sound to generalize the concept of social introversion or extroversion to all groups in which the client functions, experience in counseling seems to indicate that high scores of 60–70 or more seem to show an individual who tends to avoid people in group settings and a score below 40 is that of a client who likes to be with people in groups.

The Si score needs to be considered in combination with Mf as an indicator of conflict between a linguistic tendency in behavior (femininity) and a high Si score (social introversion); or with Pa and Sc where high scores and a low Si score (social extroversion) may reflect client desire to modify behavior through investigation of the impact of high Pa and/or Sc on functioning in a social setting. Clinical observation also leads one to question whether there is an interpretation to high K and low or high Si scores. This needs further research.

The exact items in each Clinical Scale along with other scales using the same item are shown in Dahlstrom and Welsh (1960). The amount of overlap and intercorrelations produced are also given in the same reference.

Newer MMPI Scales as shown on the National Computer Systems profile in Figure 6 have had limited use in counseling normal individuals. As can be seen from their descriptions, they have had much more usage in the clinical setting with abnormal patients. However, the counselor in a school setting needs to be aware of their potential, so they are described briefly in the following pages. There are eleven of these scales beginning with Welsh's (1956) first factor (A) of 39 items and second factor (R) of 40 items described earlier in this chapter as an indicator of anxiety and an indicator of internalization, respectively. Hathaway and Briggs (1957) discuss some of these newer scales and their normative data (A, R, Es, Dy, Rp, and Cn), but the most useful reference again is Dahlstrom and Welsh (1960).

The third scale added is Barron's (1953) Ego Strength (Es) of 68 items which are supposed to identify individuals who tend to improve more with therapy (higher score) than those who do not. A fourth is Hanvik's (1949) Low Back Pain Scale (Lb) whose 25 items are used to differentiate between veterans with a real physiological problem and those with psychosomatic problems related to pains in the back. A fifth scale is the 36 item Caudality Scale (Ca) developed by Williams (1952) and used to identify persons with "focal damage of the parietal lobe from those with frontal lobe lesions" (Hathaway and McKinley, 1951). Navran's (1954) 57-item Dependency Scale (Dy) is the sixth of the newer scales to be included. He used ratings by judges and an item analysis process to develop a scale purportedly measuring the amount of dependency present in patients who prolonged their response to therapy versus those who responded more rapidly. He also investigated differences between normals and abnormals on this scale.

The next two scales, the 28-item Dominance (Do) and the 32-item Responsibility (Re), were developed by Gough and others (1951, 1952). The Do Scale partials out persons who exhibit social initiative, persistence, and leadership skills. The Re Scale is supposed to identify persons who can assume obligations to the groups in which they function and are dependable and trustworthy. The 32-item Prejudice Scale (Pr) was also developed by Gough (1951b) to measure the psychological insecurities reflected by social prejudice manifested against minority groups. It identifies individuals with high scores who are prudish, rigid, authoritarian, and pseudo-religious. This scale is negatively related to the K Scale and the St Scale while being positively related to the F Scale and most of the Clinical Scales (except Hy). The Social Status Scale (St) of 34 items as developed by Gough (1949) tries to measure an individual's psychological conditions associated with socioeconomic class when subjects had been divided into upper and lower groups using the Sims Score Card (1927). It has a moderate correlation with the K Scale of .53 (Perlman, 1950).

The last of the newer scales is the 50-item Control Scale (Cn) developed by Cuadra (1953) in a very carefully done comparison of hospitalized patients and outpatients. He hypothesized that they would differ on control of self. Current, but limited, information indicates the items of this scale appear sensitive to the elements in self-control which identify persons who need to be confined versus those who can manage themselves under outpatient treatment.

It can be seen from the brief discussion of the last eleven scales that they are of limited use in the school setting at present. It should also be noted that they need more research to clarify their interpretation.

The item composition of each of these newer scales is shown in Dahlstrom and Welsh (1960).

The California Psychological Inventory

Construction

The *California Psychological Inventory* (CPI) is a 480-item inventory with 18 scales developed by Gough (1957, 1964) for use with normal individuals. Approximately 200 of these items were derived through research Gough has done on the MMPI and used with permission. The inventory claims two purposes. One is to develop and use behavioral descriptions with wide social and personal application among normal individuals. The other is to create scales which identify and describe the 18 variables chosen for the inventory. These variables are described in Tables 8 and 9 in terms of the ways in which they measure attributes of "social living and social interaction" for use in general counseling settings.

The instrument was selected because it uses normal individuals as its base groups and also because it illustrates what Gough (1964) has called the "empirical technique" of inventory construction. He defines a dimension of behavior (criterion) he intends to measure and then collects items pertinent to that dimension into a preliminary scale. Then using another criterion supposedly similar to the original, contrasting high and low groups on this criterion are chosen to see whether they respond to the items in the expected manner. Twelve scales were constructed in the above fashion using adjective descriptions (Gough, 1960) as the outside criterion (Do, Cs, Sy, Wb, Re, So, To, Ac, Ai, Ie, Py, and Fe). Four other scales (Sp, Sa, Sc, and Fx) were produced by internal consistency item analyses and the remaining two (Gi and Cm) were developed by special processes. Each of these scales will be discussed later.

The inventory consists of a 12-page booklet with a hand-scored, an IBM machine-scored, and a special National Computer Systems-scored answer sheet. The purchaser should specify which answer sheets he wishes. The inventory is untimed, but usually takes about 50 minutes. The last 20 items can be omitted because they are not scored on the 18 scales. There are 12 items duplicated on the answer sheet for ease in scoring.

Norms were combined by separate sexes to form a single norm group for 6000 males and for 7000 females. These are not a random sample of general population, but range widely in age, socioeconomic status and geographic distribution. The profile for males is on one side and that for females is on the reverse of the profile sheet using standard *T*-score units.

Test-retest reliabilities over a one-year interval range from .44 to .77 for 125 high school females with a median of .685 and from .38 to .75

for 101 high school males with a median of .645. For reasons discussed previously, a time interval of one year between testing raises questions about the meaning of such reliabilities. This becomes a valid question when the only other reliabilities reported are on a group of 200 prison males retested with an interval of 7 to 21 days between testings. These reliabilities ranged from .49 to .87 with a median of .80. One wonders whether the higher reliabilities of the last group are produced by less personality change between testings or because an older group manifests more stable behavior.

Validities vary in terms of the vagueness or specificity of the criteria available for a given scale. In general, the criteria were correlations of ratings of an appropriate group with their scores on a given scale or the use of ratings to identify a group outstanding in behavior associated with a given scale and then testing the significance of the difference between their scores and an unselected sample. In each of the latter cases, significant critical ratios were found. Because Gough's "empirical method" involves construction of a series of items to measure a given behavioral concept, a form of construct validity is inherent in the above process.

Another approach to validity is by use of factor analysis. Factorial studies by Crites, et al. (1961), Gowan (1958), Hicks (1960), Mitchell and Pierce-Jones (1960), Nichols and Schnell (1963), and Springob and Struening (1964) are listed as references to be followed up by the reader. In general they show that four or five factors can account for a major proportion of the variance of the 18 CPI scales with general agreement on two factors represented by the scales in Class I and Class II: 1) personal adjustment and social poise, and 2) extroversion or gregariousness.

Jackson (1960) discusses the effect of response set on validity of CPI scores.

Still a third type of validity is found in the intercorrelations of the 18 scales of the inventory and in correlation of its scales with those of the SVIB, MMPI, GZTS, EPPS, and Cattell 16 PF Inventory which are reported in Gough (1964). A fourth type of validity is represented by the profile means and standard deviations for various academic and occupational groups in the above reference.

These varied evidences of validity seem to indicate that Gough's method of constructing the inventory was a productive one and that it offers promise for counseling use limited at present by lack of more specific evidence of reliabilities.

Limited evidence of readability exists. Research by Gough (1964) seems to show use from Grade 9 up is appropriate. Below that level, some items are "difficult and a few are without relevance."

TABLE 8

Description of first eleven scales of the California Psychological Inventory.

HIGH SCORERS Tend to be seen as:	SCALE AND PURPOSE	LOW SCORERS Tend to be seen as:
	CLASS I. MEASURES OF POISE, ASCENDANCY, AND SELF-ASSURANCE	
Aggressive, confident, persistent, and planful; as being persuasive and verbally fluent; as self-reliant and independent; and as having leadership potential and initiative.	1. Do (dominance) To assess factors of leadership ability, dominance, persistence, and social initiative.	Retiring, inhibited, commonplace, indifferent, silent and unassuming; as being slow in thought and action; as avoiding of situations of tension and decision; and as lacking in self-confidence.
Ambitious, active, forceful, insightful, resourceful, and versatile; as being ascendant and self-seeking; effective in communication; and as having personal scope and breadth of interests.	2. Cs (capacity for status) To serve as an index of an individual's capacity for status (not his actual or achieved status). The scale attempts to measure the personal qualities and attributes which underlie and lead to status.	Apathetic, shy, conventional dull, mild, simple, and slow; as being stereotyped in thinking; restricted in outlook and interests; and as being uneasy and awkward in new or unfamiliar social situations.
Outgoing, enterprising, and ingenious; as being competitive and forward; and as original and fluent in thought.	3. Sy (sociability) To identify persons of outgoing, sociable, participative temperament.	Awkward, conventional, quiet, submissive, and unassuming; as being detached and passive in attitude; and as being suggestible and overly influenced by others' reactions and opinions.
Clever, enthusiastic, imaginative, quick, informal, spontaneous, and talkative; as being active and vigorous; and as having an expressive, ebullient nature.	4. Sp (social presence) To assess factors such as poise, spontaneity, and self-confidence in personal and social interaction.	Deliberate, moderate, patient, self-restrained, and simple; as vacillating and uncertain in decision; and as being literal and unoriginal in thinking and judging.
Intelligent, outspoken, sharp-witted, demanding, aggressive, and self-centered; as being persuasive and verbally fluent; and as possessing self-confidence and self-assurance.	5. Sa (self-acceptance) To assess factors such as sense of personal worth, self-acceptance, and capacity for independent thinking and action.	Methodical, conservative, dependable, conventional, easygoing, and quiet; as self-abasing and given to feelings of guilt and self-blame; and as being passive in action and narrow in interests.
Energetic, enterprising, alert, ambitious, and versatile; as being productive and active; and as valuing work and effort for its own sake.	6. Wb (sense of well-being) To identify persons who minimize their worries and complaints, and who are relatively free from self-doubt and disillusionment.	Unambitious, leisurely, awkward, cautious, apathetic, and conventional; as being self-defensive and apologetic; and as constricted in thought and action.
	CLASS II. MEASURES OF SOCIALIZATION, MATURITY, AND RESPONSIBILITY	
Planful, responsible, thorough, progressive, capable, dignified, and independent; as being conscientious and dependable; resourceful and efficient; and as being alert to ethical and moral issues.	7. Re (responsibility) To identify persons of conscientious, responsible, and dependable disposition and temperament.	Immature, moody, lazy, awkward, changeable, and disbelieving; as being influenced by personal bias, spite, and dogmatism; and as under-controlled and impulsive in behavior.
Serious, honest, industrious, modest, obliging, sincere, and steady; as being conscientious and responsible; and as being self-denying and conforming.	8. So (socialization) To indicate the degree of social maturity, integrity, and rectitude which the individual has attained.	Defensive, demanding, opinionated, resentful, stubborn, headstrong, rebellious, and undependable; as being guileful and deceitful in dealing with others; and as given to excess, exhibition, and ostentation in their behavior.
Calm, patient, practical, slow, self-denying, inhibited, thoughtful, and deliberate; as being strict and thorough in their own work and in their expectations for others; and as being honest and conscientious.	9. Sc (self-control) To assess the degree and adequacy of self-regulation and self-control and freedom from impulsivity and self-centeredness.	Impulsive, shrewd, excitable, irritable, self-centered, and uninhibited; as being aggressive and assertive; and as overemphasizing personal pleasure and self-gain.
Enterprising, informal, quick, tolerant, clear-thinking, and resourceful; as being intellectually able and verbally fluent; and as having broad and varied interests.	10. To (tolerance) To identify persons with permissive, accepting, and non-judgmental social beliefs and attitude.	Suspicious, narrow, aloof, wary, and retiring; as being passive and overly judgmental in attitude; and as disbelieving and distrustful in personal and social outlook.
Co-operative, enterprising, outgoing, sociable warm, and helpful; as being concerned with making a good impression; and as being diligent and persistent.	11. Gi (good impression) To identify persons capable of creating a favorable impression, and who are concerned about how others react to them.	Inhibited, cautious, shrewd, wary, aloof, and resentful; as being cool and distant in their relationships with others; and as being self-centered and too little concerned with the needs and wants of others.

TABLE 9

Description of last seven scales of the California Psychological Inventory.

HIGH SCORERS Tend to be seen as:	SCALE AND PURPOSE	LOW SCORERS Tend to be seen as:
CLASS II. MEASURES OF SOCIALIZATION, MATURITY, AND RESPONSIBILITY (Continued)		
Dependable, moderate, tactful, reliable, sincere, patient, steady, and realistic; as being honest and conscientious; and as having common sense and good judgment.	12. Cm (communality) To indicate the degree to which an individual's reactions and responses correspond to the model ("common") pattern established for the inventory.	Impatient, changeable, complicated, imaginative, disorderly, nervous, restless, and confused; as being guileful and deceitful; inattentive and forgetful; and as having internal conflicts and problems.
CLASS III. MEASURES OF ACHIEVEMENT POTENTIAL AND INTELLECTUAL EFFICIENCY		
Capable, co-operative, efficient, organized, responsible, stable, and sincere; as being persistent and industrious; and as valuing intellectual activity and intellectual achievement.	13. Ac (achievement via conformance). To identify those factors of interest and motivation which facilitate achievement in any setting where conformance is a positive behavior.	Coarse, stubborn, aloof, awkward, insecure, and opinionated; as easily disorganized under stress or pressures to conform; and as pessimistic about their occupational futures.
Mature, forceful, strong, dominant, demanding, and foresighted; as being independent and self-reliant; and as having superior intellectual ability and judgment.	14. Ai (achievement via independence) To identify those factors of interest and motivation which facilitate achievement in any setting where autonomy and independence are positive behaviors.	Inhibited, anxious, cautious, dissatisfied, dull, and wary; as being submissive and compliant before authority; and as lacking in self-insight and self-understanding.
Efficient, clear-thinking, capable, intelligent, progressive, planful, thorough, and resourceful; as being alert and well-informed; and as placing a high value on cognitive and intellectual matters.	15. Ie (intellectual efficiency) To indicate the degree of personal and intellectual efficiency which the individual has attained.	Cautious, confused, easygoing, defensive, shallow, and unambitious; as being conventional and stereotyped in thinking; and as lacking in self-direction and self-discipline.
CLASS IV. MEASURES OF INTELLECTUAL AND INTEREST MODES		
Observant, spontaneous, quick, perceptive, talkative, resourceful, and changeable; as being verbally fluent and socially ascendant; and as being rebellious toward rules, restrictions, and constraints.	16. Py (psychological-mindedness) To measure the degree to which the individual is interested in, and responsive to, the inner needs, motives, and experiences of others.	Apathetic, peaceable, serious, cautious, and unassuming; as being slow and deliberate in tempo; and as being overly conforming and conventional.
Insightful, informal, adventurous, confident, humorous, rebellious, idealistic, assertive, and egoistic; as being sarcastic and cynical; and as highly concerned with personal pleasure and diversion.	17. Fx (flexibility) To indicate the degree of flexibility and adaptability of a person's thinking and social behavior.	Deliberate, cautious, worrying, industrious, guarded, mannerly, methodical, and rigid; as being formal and pedantic in thought; and as being overly deferential to authority, custom, and tradition.
Appreciative, patient, helpful, gentle, moderate, persevering, and sincere; as being respectful and accepting of others; and as behaving in a conscientious and sympathetic way.	18. Fe (femininity) To assess the masculinity or femininity of interests. (High scores indicate more feminine interests, low scores more masculine.)	Outgoing, hard-headed, ambitious, masculine, active, robust, and restless; as being manipulative and opportunistic in dealing with others; blunt and direct in thinking and action; and impatient with delay, indecision, and reflection.

Interpretation

There are three validating scales in the CPI. The first of these is the Well-being Scale (Wb). Its purpose is to show persons whose low scores represent an underestimate of their well-being and who "exaggerate their worries and misfortunes as distinguished from those who present a relatively accurate and objective picture of their concerns and problems" (Gough, 1964). Responses of hospitalized psychoneurotics were contrasted with responses of a group instructed to answer as if they had serious internal conflicts. Psychoneurotic patients scored below average, but lowest scores on the Wb scale were secured by those instructed to fake poor scores. So the extremely low Wb score is considered that of a possible malingerer or "test faker."

The second validating score is the Good Impression Scale (Gi). This scale was developed by having a group answer potential items normally once and answer another time with instructions to present the best picture of themselves that they could. The items showing the greatest change became the Gi Scale. Gough (1964) warns that moderate scores, such as those in the top half of the average group, describe individuals who create a good impression because they are more cooperative, adaptable, and outgoing. Very high scores represent possible faked or invalid scores, or (perhaps more likely) are attained by individuals who are manipulative and indifferent to the feelings of others.

The third validating scale is the Communality score (Cm). The 28 items of this scale represented a high degree of response agreement in all the original normative samples. Each item is one on which nearly all respondents answer the same way (either agree or disagree); hence, those who secured *scores below 25* either did not understand the instructions, were careless, answered randomly, or (possibly) deviated from the conventional mold in a valid and hence diagnostic way.

Gough claims the CPI is not easy to fake because it contains many subtle items and because in the initial scale construction good-impression and other response sets were automatically placed under control. (For a discussion of subtle versus obvious items, see Wiener, 1948). Gough (1964) presents mean profiles of deliberately faked and randomly answered inventory administrations which support the statements above concerning Wb and Cm. The "faked good" profiles offer moderate support for his contentions about Gi.

The other 15 scales are interpreted in terms of three approaches. The first would involve meaning of each scale by itself. The second considers interaction between and among the scales, such as two-scale analysis (Heilbrun, et al., 1962). The third phase of interpretation is profile analysis. There are four groupings of individual scales referred to as "classes" of scales.

Class I, in addition to the Wb scale, has five other scales dealing with feelings of interpersonal and intrapersonal competence as shown by measures of "poise, ascendancy, and self-assurance."

The Dominance Scale (Do) attempts to evaluate elements of leadership, persistence, and social initiative. As shown in Table 8, high scores reflect the person who is aggressive, persistent, self-reliant, and persuasive, while low scores describe a person who is retiring, slow, silent, and who lacks self-confidence. The opposite poles of this scale represent the dominance-submission behavior included in a number of personality inventories.

The Capacity for Status Scale (Cs) is an index of a person's potential to achieve status. High scores characterize the ambitious, insightful, resourceful, and versatile person who relates well to others; low scores show an individual who is apathetic, inhibited, awkward in new social settings, and who thinks in stereotypes.

The Sociability Scale (Sy) shows an individual who is outgoing and sociable. Other adjectives used to describe the high scorer are competitive, ingenious, original, and fluent in thinking. The low scorer is described as awkward, conventional, passive, and easily influenced by others. This scale differs from the Socialization Scale (So) in Class II in that the latter reflects a responsible, sincere interest in the welfare of others, while the Sy Scale is more a self-seeking, egocentric, or self-satisfying attribute involving others. Perhaps they could be distinguished as "manipulating others" versus "serving others."

The Social Presence Scale (Sp) measures poise and self-confidence in social relations. High scores are described as vigorous, spontaneous, and expressive, while those with low scores are considered patient, self-restrained, vacillating, and literal-minded.

The fifth scale is Self-Acceptance (Sa), evaluating personal or self-worth and capacity for independence. Individuals with high scores are intelligent, sharp-witted, and self-assured. Those with low scores are methodical, quiet, self-abasing, and narrow in interests.

The sixth scale, Wb, has been discussed previously as a validating scale. Moderately high scores reflect persons who play down worries and complaints and are free from self-doubt. Low scores are made by persons who are self-defensive, apathetic, apologetic, and constricted.

Gough describes scores in *Class II* as showing concern with social norms and values. In addition to Gi and Cm discussed previously, there are four other variables in this group.

The first is the Responsibility Scale (Re), which attempts to show those who are conscientious and dependable. High scorers are thorough, capable, independent, and efficient, while low scorers are immature, changeable, biased, dogmatic, and impulsive.

Scale 8 is the Sociability Scale (So), reflecting an interest in social relations focusing on welfare of others. Those with high scores are modest, obliging, conscientious, and self-denying. Those with low scores are defensive, demanding, headstrong, rebellious, and ostentatious.

The ninth scale is Self-Control (Sc), measuring the amount of self-regulation and freedom from impulsive behavior present in an individual.

The tenth scale is Tolerance (To), identifying clients who are permissive and accepting of others.

The eleventh scale, Gi, and twelfth scale, Cm, have been discussed before and need no further description.

Class III contains three variables related to academic performance: Ac (achievement by conformity), Ai (achievement through independence), and Ie (intellectual efficiency).

The Ac Scale indicates achievement behavior which meets the expectations of social groups, such as the school faculty, parents, or community groups. A high score identifies the respondent who is capable, efficient, and industrious. A low score is said to describe the respondent who is easily disorganized and vocationally uncertain.

The Ai Scale, as its name indicates, shows a person whose motivation is toward achieving according to his goals rather than those of others. The high scorer is mature, forceful, and self-reliant. The low scorer is dissatisfied, submissive, and has poor self-insight.

The Ie score reflects the amount of personal and intellectual efficiency possessed by the respondent. The high scorer places considerable value on intellectual pursuits, while the low scorer is stereotyped in thinking and shallow.

It should be noted that all three measures in Class III are affective or motivational reactions to cognitive situations, *not* measures of aptitude or ability.

Class IV contains three assorted measures of psychological behavior. The Psychological-Mindedness Scale (Py) might better have been named "Sensitivity to Others." The Flexibility Scale (Fx) shows how easily a respondent's behavior adapts to changing conditions. The Femininity Scale (Fe) shows the respondent with high scores as having feminine interests, with low scores indicating masculine interests.

The second phase of interpretation focuses on interaction between scales as shown by Figure 7. Here each quadrant, as represented by one of the four possible combinations of the Do and Sy scales, reflects the social interactive behavior described by the adjectives in that

FIGURE 7

Two-scale analysis of the Dominance (Do) and Sociability (Sy) scales of the *California Psychological Inventory*

From the standpoint of social technique and small group process theory, the interaction of the Do (dominance) and Sy (sociability) scales is of some interest; the typical correlation between these two scales is +.65. The predictions for their interaction are these:

EXPECTED BEHAVIORS

Do high

analyzes	advises
criticizes	coordinates
disapproves	directs
judges	leads
resists	initiates

Sy low ———————————————————————— Sy high

avoids (evades)	acquiesces
concedes	agrees
relinquishes	assists
retreats	cooperates
withdraws	obliges

Do low

quadrant; i.e., Do high — Sy low shows the person who "analyzes, criticizes, disapproves, judges, and resists" in social settings (Gough, 1964).

The third phase of interpretation centers about profile analysis. The main points Gough recommends are (1964):

1. That the counselor note the overall elevation of the profile. The majority of scores above a *T*-score of 50 indicate effective adjustment; those below this point show possible adjustment problems.

2. Look for high or low classes of scales.

3. List the highest and lowest scales.

4. Identify profile elements which describe the respondent as different from most other profiles.

5. Consider how the profile for a given individual may be unique to him rather than comparing him to the normative group.

The Guilford-Zimmerman Temperament Survey

Construction

The *Guilford-Zimmerman Temperament Survey* (GZTS) is an excellent example of an inventory whose construction is based on factor analytic methods and how statisticians can provide an inventory easy to administer and to score. It is also an excellent example of how *not* to label or name scales to be used directly by a counselor with a client.

The GZTS was constructed by a factor analysis used to refine the factors of the three Guilford-Martin inventories: GAMIN, STDCR, and the *Personnel Inventory* (O, Ag, Co). This factor analysis produced the ten-scale bipolar GZTS. The items of this inventory use the second person pronoun and are affirmative statements marked *yes, no,* or left blank. If more than four of the thirty items in each scale are left blank, that scale is invalidated. There are few, if any, objectionable items on these scales.

The GZTS is easy to administer, to score, and to profile. It consists of ten traits of 30 items each (300 items). The answer sheet is unique because it is numbered across rather than vertically. There are five items in each row and thirty rows on each side of the answer sheet. Every fifth item is scored on the same scale, so that when a scoring template is placed over the answer sheet, the marked items in each column are the score for that scale. The front of the answer sheet covers scales G, R, A, S, E and the back of the sheet includes scales O, F, T, P, M. These are described as follows, with the high score meaning first:

G — General Activity. Strong drive, activity, and energy vs. slowness and inefficiency.

R — Restraint. Seriousness, persistence, and control vs. impulsiveness and happy-go-lucky behavior.

A — Ascendance. Persuasiveness and leadership vs. submissiveness.

S — Sociability. Ease with others and social participation vs. shyness, withdrawal, and reserve.

E — Emotional Stability. Optimism, cheerfulness, and stability vs. neurotic tendencies, pessimism, and depression.

O — Objectivity. Lack of egoism vs. touchiness or hypersensitivity.

F — Friendliness. Acceptance and respect for others vs. hostility and self-centeredness.

T — Thoughtfulness. Reflectiveness and interest in cognitive pursuits vs. interest in environmental interaction and lack of tact.

P — Personal relations. Getting along with people vs. belligerence and intolerance or suspiciousness of others.

M — Masculinity. Interest in masculine activities vs. femininity of interest.

It takes about one minute to score the inventory. An estimate of range of scores if items are omitted is possible by adding the omitted items to the obtained score and explaining to the client that his actual score is somewhere between his obtained score and this score with omitted items added to it. He can never score lower than his obtained score, nor higher than this adjusted score.

Scores are separated into C-score units and percentiles on the profile, which poses a problem of translating to T-score approximations.

Reliabilities for the scales were computed by Kuder-Richardson and split-half methods. They are reported as one set of "consensus" reliabilities ranging from .75 to .87, with a median of .80. Stability of these scores is also discussed by Jackson (1961) in an article including many correlational GZTS references.

Validity is inherent in construction which used two succeeding factor analyses (Guilford-Martin and Guilford-Zimmerman) combined with internal consistency item analysis (which is really reliability). A table of intercorrelations is presented in the manual (Guilford and Zimmerman, 1949) which shows highest correlations all positive to be R with T, .42; A with S, .61, and A with O, .41; E with O, .69; O with P, .43; and F with P, .50. The only significant sex differences are reported for the Masculinity Scale, although the A and F Scales also show sex differences on the profile.

Interpretation

The meaning of the scales seems clearly indicated by the scale names and descriptions listed above and will not be repeated here. The problem for the counselor is that the names of these opposite poles on the profile are the ones listed above, and unless names more acceptable to the client are used, he cannot be shown the profile. If he is shown the profile, the counselor has to describe "Impulsiveness," "Shyness," "Submissiveness," "Emotional instability," "Hypersensitiveness," "Hostility," and "Intolerance."

In general, a profile with all high scores reflects a "faked good" performance and all low scores usually indicate serious psychological problems.

Conclusion

The three structured personality inventories described in this chapter represent different approaches to measuring behavior and considerable differences in construction. For a much more complete list of such inventories and critical reviews by competent professionals, the reader is referred to the chapter on "Character and Personality Tests — Nonprojective" in the various editions of Buros (1965).

BIBLIOGRAPHY

Allport, G. W., Vernon, P. E., and Lindzey, G., *Study of Values: Manual of Directions*. Boston: Houghton Mifflin, 1951.

American Psychological Association, *Standards for Educational and Psychological Tests and Manuals*. Washington: APA, 1950.

————, *Standards for Educational and Psychological Tests and Manuals*. Washington: APA, 1966a.

————, "Testimony before the House Special Committee on Invasion of Privacy of the Committee on Government Operations." *American Psychologist*, Vol. 21, 1966b.

Barron, F., "An ego-strength scale which predicts response to psychotherapy." *Journal of Consulting Psychology*, Vol. 17, 1953.

Block, J., *The Challenge of Response Sets*. New York: Appleton-Century-Crofts, 1965.

Bordin, E. S., "A theory of vocational interest as dynamic phenomena." *Educational and Psychological Measurement*, Vol. 3, 1943.

Brayfield, A. N., "Testimony before the Senate Subcommittee on Constitutional Rights of the Committee on the Judiciary." *American Psychologist*, Vol. 20, 1965.

Buros, Oscar K., *The Sixth Mental Measurements Yearbook*. Highland Park, New Jersey: Gryphon Press, 1965.

Carter, H. D., "The development of vocational attitudes." *Journal of Consulting Psychology*, Vol. 4, 1940.

Clark, K. E., *Vocational Interests of Nonprofessional Men*. Minneapolis: University of Minnesota Press, 1961.

————, and Campbell, D. P., *Minnesota Vocational Interest Inventory Manual*. New York: The Psychological Corporation, 1965.

Clemans, W. V., "An index of item-criterion relationship." *Educational and Psychological Measurement*, Vol. 18, 1958.

Cofer, C. N., Chance, June E., and Judson, A. J., "A study of malingering on the MMPI." *Journal of Psychology*, Vol. 27, 1949.

Cottle, W. C., *A Factorial Study of the Multiphasic, Strong, Kuder and Bell Inventories Using a Population of Adult Males*. Unpublished D. Ed. dissertation, Syracuse University, 1949.

————, "A factorial study of the Multiphasic, Strong, Kuder and Bell inventories using a population of adult males." *Psychometrika*, Vol. 15, 1950a.

————, "Card versus booklet forms of the MMPI. *Journal of Applied Psychology*, Vol. 34, 1950b.

————, *Manual for the School Interest Inventory*. Boston: Houghton Mifflin Co., 1966.

————, and Downie, N. M., *Procedures and Preparation for Counseling*. Englewood Cliffs, New Jersey: Prentice-Hall, Inc., 1960.

————, and Powell, J. O., "The effect of random answers to the MMPI." *Educational and Psychological Measurement*, Vol. 11, 1951.

————, "Relationship of mean scores on the Strong, Kuder and Bell Inventories with the MMPI M-F Scale as a criterion." *Trans. Kansas Academy of Science*. Vol. 52, 1949.

Crites, J. O., *et al.*, "A factor analysis of the California Psychological Inventory." *Journal of Applied Psychology*, Vol. 45, 1961.

Cuodra, C. A., *A Psychometric Investigation of Control Factors in Psychological Adjustment*. Unpublished Ph.D. dissertation, University of California, 1953.

Dahlstrom, W. G., "Commentary: The roles of social desirability and acquiescence in responses to the MMPI." In Messick, S., and Ross, J., *Measurement in Personality and Cognition*. New York, John Wiley and Sons, 1962.

————, and Welsh, G. S., *An MMPI Handbook: A Guide to Clinical Practices and Research*. Minneapolis: University of Minnesota Press, 1960.

D'Arcy, P. F., *Constancy of Interest Factor Patterns Within the Specific Vocation of a Foreign Missionary*. Dissertation, Catholic University of America Studies in Psychology and Psychiatry, Vol. 9, 1954.

Darley, J. G., *Clinical Aspects and Interpretation of the Strong Vocational Interest Blank*. New York: The Psychological Corporation, 1941.

————, and Hagenah, Theda, *Vocational Interest Measurement*. Minneapolis: University of Minnesota Press, 1955.

————, and McNamara, W. J., *Manual for the Minnesota Personality Scale*. New York: The Psychological Corporation, 1943.

Downie, N. M., *Fundamentals of Measurement, Second Edition*. New York: Oxford University Press, 1967.

Drake, L. E., "A social I. E. scale for the MMPI." *Journal of Applied Psychology*, Vol. 40, 1946.

————, and Oetting, E. R., *An MMPI Codebook for Counselors*. Minneapolis: University of Minnesota Press, 1959.

Edwards, A. L., *Manual for the Personal Preference Schedule*. New York: The Psychological Corporation, 1954, 1959.

————, and Thurstone, L. L., "An internal consistency check for scale values determined by the method of successive intervals." *Psychometrika*, Vol. 17, 1953.

Ellis, A., "Recent research with personality questionnaires." *Journal of Consulting Psychology,* Vol. 17, 1953.

Forbes, F. W., and Cottle, W. C., "A New Method for Determining Readability of Standardized Tests." *Journal of Applied Psychology,* Vol. 37, 1953.

Fredericksen, N., "Response set scores as predictors of performance." *Personnel Psychology,* Vol. 18, 1965.

Fryer, D., *The Measurement of Interests in Relation to Human Adjustment.* New York: Henry Holt and Co., 1931.

Gough, H. G., "A new dimension of status: III. Discrepancies between the St scale and 'objective' status." *American Sociological Review,* Vol. 14, 1949.

————, "The F minus K dissimulation index for the MMPI." *Journal of Consulting Psychology,* Vol. 14, 1950.

————, "Studies of social intolerance: II. A personality scale for anti-Semitism." *Journal of Social Psychology,* Vol. 33, 1951a.

————, "The Adjective Checklist as a personality assessment research technique." *Psychological Reports,* Vol. 6, 1960.

————, *Manual for the California Psychological Inventory.* Palo Alto, California: Consulting Psychologists Press, 1956.

————, *Manual for the California Psychological Inventory, Revised.* Palo Alto, California: Consulting Psychologists Press, 1964.

————, *et al.,* "A personality scale for dominance." *Journal of Abnormal and Social Psychology,* Vol. 46, 1951b.

————, "A personality scale for social responsibility." *Journal of Abnormal and Social Psychology,* Vol. 47, 1952.

Gowan, J. C., "Intercorrelations and factor analysis of tests given to teaching candidates." *Journal of Experimental Education,* Vol. 27, 1958.

Guilford, J. P., and Zimmerman, W. S., *Manual for the Guilford-Zimmerman Temperament Survey.* Beverly Hills, California: Sheridan Supply, 1949.

Guthrie, G. M., "Six MMPI diagnostic profiles." *Journal of Psychology,* Vol. 30, 1950.

Hahn, M. E., *Psychoevaluation.* New York: McGraw-Hill, 1963.

————, *Planning Ahead After 40.* Beverly Hills, California: Western Psychological Services, 1967.

————, and MacLean, *Counseling Psychology.* New York: McGraw-Hill, 1955.

Hanvik, L. J., *Some Psychological Dimensions of Low Back Pain.* Unpublished Ph.D. dissertation. University of Minnesota, 1949.

Harris, R. W., and Lingoes, J. C., "Subscales of the MMPI: An aid to profile interpretation." Mimeographed report. Department of Psychiatry, University of California, 1955.

Hathaway, S. R., "A coding system for MMPI profiles." *Journal of Consulting Psychology*, Vol. 11, 1947.

———, and Briggs, P. F., "Some normative data on new MMPI scales." *Journal of Clinical Psychology*, Vol. 13, 1957.

Hathaway, S. R., and McKinley, J. C., *Manual: The Minnesota Multiphasic Personality Inventory*. New York: The Psychological Corporation, 1943.

———, *Manual: The Minnesota Multiphasic Personality Inventory, Revised*. New York: The Psychological Corporation, 1951.

Hathaway, S. R., and Meehl, P. E., *An Atlas for the Clinical Use of the MMPI*. Minneapolis: University of Minnesota Press, 1951.

Heilbrun, A. B., Jr., *et al.*, "The validity of two-scale pattern interpretation on the California Psychological Inventory." *Journal of Applied Psychology*, Vol. 46, 1962.

Hicks, R. A., *Factor Analytic Studies of the California Psychological Inventory*. Unpublished Master's thesis, San Jose State College, California, 1960.

Holland, J., *Psychology of Vocational Choice*. Boston: Blaisdell Press, 1966.

Jackson, D. N., "Stylistic response determinants in the California Psychological Inventory." *Educational and Psychological Measurement*, Vol. 20, 1960.

Jackson, J. M., "The stability of Guilford-Zimmerman personality measures." *Journal of Applied Psychology*, Vol. 45, 1961.

Kleinmutz, B., "MMPI decision rules for the identification of college maladjustment: A digital computer approach." *Psychological Monographs*, Vol. 77, 1963.

Koponen, A., *The influence of demographic factors on responses to the Edwards Personal Preference Schedule*. Unpublished Ph.D. dissertation, Columbia University, 1957.

Kriedt, P. H., "Vocational interests of psychologists." *Journal of Applied Psychology*, Vol. 33, 1949.

Kuder, G. F., *General Interest Survey Manual*. Chicago: Science Research Associates, 1964.

———, *Manual for the Kuder Preference Record-Vocational Form B*. Chicago: Science Research Associates, 1946.

———, *Occupational Interest Survey General Manual*. Chicago: Science Research Associates, 1966.

Lebensohn, Z. M., "Testomony before the Senate Subcommittee on Constitutional Rights of the Committee on the Judiciary." *American Psychologist*, Vol. 20, 1965.

Lee, E. E., and Thorpe, L. A., *Manual for the Occupational Interest Inventory — Advanced Series*. Los Angeles: California Test Bureau, 1943.

Mallinson, G. G., and Crumrine, W. M., "An investigation of the stability of interests of high school students." *Journal of Educational Research*, Vol. 45, 1952.

Menninger, K., "Testimony before the Senate Subcommittee on Constitutional Rights of the Committee on the Judiciary." *American Psychologist,* Vol. 20, 1965.

Mitchell, J. V., Jr., and Pierce-Jones, J., "A factor analysis of Gough's California Psychological Inventory." *Journal of Consulting Psychology,* Vol. 24, 1960.

Murray, H. A., *et al., Explorations in Personality.* New York: Oxford University Press, 1938.

Navran, L., "A rationally derived MMPI scale to measure dependence." *Journal of Consulting Psychology,* Vol. 18, 1954.

Nichols, R. C., and Schnell, R. R., "Factor scales for the California Psychological Inventory." *Journal of Consulting Psychology,* Vol. 27, 1963.

Norman, W. T., "A spatial analysis of an interest domain." *Educational and Psychological Measurement,* Vol. 20, 1960.

Olheiser, Sister Mary David, O.S.B., *Development of a Sister-Teacher Interest Scale for the Strong Vocational Interest Blank for Women.* Unpublished Ph.D. dissertation, Boston College, 1962.

Perlman, M., *Social class membership and test-taking attitude.* Unpublished Master's thesis, University of Chicago, 1950.

Rosen, A., "Stability of the new MMPI scales and statistical procedures for evaluating changes and differences in psychiatric patients." *Journal of Consulting Psychology,* Vol. 30, 1966.

Rothney, J. M. W., "Reviews of the SVIB and MVII." *Journal of Counseling Psychology,* Vol. 14, 1967.

Ruebhausen, O. M., and Brim, O. G., Jr., "Privacy and behavioral research." *American Psychologist,* Vol. 21, 1966.

Schmidt, H. O., "Test profiles as a diagnostic aid: The MMPI." *Journal of Applied Psychology,* Vol. 29, 1945.

Schwebel, M., *The Interests of Pharmacists.* New York: Kings Crown Press, 1951.

Simon, E., and Hales, W. M., "Note on a suicide key in the MMPI." *American Journal of Psychiatry,* Vol. 106, 1949.

Sims, V. M., *Sims Score Card for Socio-Economic Status.* Bloomington, Illinois: Public School Publishing Co., 1927.

Smith, K., "Testimony before the Senate Subcommittee on Constitutional Rights of the Committee of the Judiciary." *American Psychologist,* Vol. 20, 1965.

Springob, H. K., and Struening, E. L., "A factor analysis of the California Psychological Inventory on a high school population." *Journal of Counseling Psychology,* Vol. 11, 1964.

Strong, E. K., Jr., *Manual: Strong Vocational Interest Blanks* (T399 and Women's 1946 Form). Revised by David P. Campbell. Stanford, California: Stanford University Press, 1966.

———, *Vocational Interests 18 Years After College.* Minneapolis: University of Minnesota Press, 1955.

————, *Vocational Interests of Men and Women.* Palo Alto, California: Stanford University Press, 1943.

————, *Manual for Strong Vocational Interest Blanks for Men and Women,* Revised Blanks (Forms M and W). Palo Alto, California: Consulting Psychologists Press, 1959.

————, and Tucker, A. C., "The use of vocational interest scales in planning a medical career." *Psychological Monographs,* Vol. 66, 1952.

————, *et al., The 1966 Revision of the Strong Vocational Interest Blank for Men.* Stanford, California: Stanford University Press, 1966.

Super, D. E., *Appraising Vocational Fitness.* New York: Harper and Brothers, 1949.

————, and Crites, J. O., *Appraising Vocational Fitness, Revised Edition.* New York: Harper and Brothers, 1962.

Terman, L. M., "Scientists and non-scientists in a group of 800 gifted men." *Psychological Monographs,* Vol. 68, 1954.

————, and Miles, Catherine C., *Sex and Personality.* New York: McGraw-Hill, 1936.

Thorndike, E. L., *Thorndike Century Junior Dictionary.* New York: Scott, Foresman, and Co., 1942.

Tutton, Marie E., "Stability of adolescent vocational interests. *Vocational Guidance Quarterly,* Vol. 3, 1955.

Tyler, L. E., "Work and individual differences." In Borow, H., *Man in a World at Work.* Boston: Houghton Mifflin, 1964.

Veldman, D. J., and Pierce-Jones, J., "Sex differences in factor structure for the California Psychological Inventory." *Journal of Consulting Psychology,* Vol. 28, 1964.

Weingarten, K. P., *Picture Interest Inventory.* Los Angeles: California Test Bureau, 1958.

Welsh, G. S., "An anxiety index and an internalization ratio for the MMPI." *Journal of Consulting Psychology,* Vol. 16, 1952.

————, "An extension of Hathaway's MMPI coding system." *Journal of Consulting Psychology,* Vol. 12, 1948.

————, "Factor dimensions A and R." In Welsh, G. S., and Dahlstrom, W. G., *Basic Readings on the MMPI in Psychology and Medicine.* Minneapolis: University of Minnesota Press, 1956.

————, "Some practical uses of MMPI profile coding." *Journal of Consulting Psychology,* Vol. 15, 1951.

Wheeler, W. M., *et al.,* "The internal structure of the MMPI." *Journal of Consulting Psychology,* Vol. 15, 1951.

Wiener, D. N., "Subtle and obvious keys for the MMPI." *Journal of Consulting Psychology,* Vol. 12, 1948.

Williams, H. L., "The development of a caudality scale for the MMPI." *Journal of Clinical Psychology,* Vol. 8, 1952.

INDEX

Allport, G. W., Vernon, P. E., and Lindzey, G., 46, 67–69
Allport, Vernon, Lindzey Study of Values, 67–69
  construction, 67–69
  interpretation, 69
  ipsative scores, 69
  reading level, 10, 68
  reliabilities, 68
  scales, 68
  Spranger's types, 68–69
  validities, 68
American Psychological Association, 19, 23, 25
American Psychiatric Association, 23, 25
Barron, F., 82, 95
Bell Adjustment Inventory, 3, 4, 39, 42, 76–78
Bernreuter Personality Inventory, 3, 78
Block, J., 73, 75
Bordin, E. S., 32, 46
Borow, H., 48
Brayfield, A. N., 23–25, 28
Buros, O. K., 78, 105
California Psychological Inventory
  construction, 96–99
  correlation with other inventories, 97
  empirical technique, 96–97
  factor analysis, 97
  intercorrelation of scales, 97
  interpretation, 100–103
  norms, 96
  potential, 80
  profile analysis, 103
  readability, 97
  reliabilities, 96–97
  scales, 100–103
    class I, 101
    class II, 101–102
    class III, 102
    class IV, 102–103

  subtle items, 100
  two-scale analysis, 103
  validities, 97
  validating scales, 100
California Test of Personality, 78–79
Carter, H. D., 46
Clark, K. E., 3
Clark, K. E., and Campbell, D. P., 32
Clemens, W. V., 57
Cofer, C. N., *et al.*, 27, 84, 86
Comrey, A., 86
Cottle, W. C., 2, 5, 6, 31, 32, 33, 39, 47, 48, 73, 76, 77, 85, 86
  and Downie, N. M., 30, 48
  and Powell, J. O., 39, 73–74
Cowdery, K. M., 51
Crites, J. O., *et al.*, 97
Cuodra, C. A., 82, 95
Dahlstrom, W. G., 75
  and Welsh, G. S., 6, 76, 82, 86, 88, 89, 90, 91, 92, 93, 94, 95
D'Arcy, Rev. P. F., 31, 47, 48
Darley, J. G., 46
  and Hagenah, Theda, 2, 46
  and McNamara, W. J., 5
Downie, N. M., 78
Drake, L. E., 82, 94
  and Oetting, E. R., 84
Edwards, A. L., 6, 7, 63–67, 88
Edwards Personal Preference Schedule
  consistency scale and score, 63
  construction, 63–64
  interpretation, 64–67
  ipsative scores, 67
  names of scales, 64–66
  norms, 64, 67
  reading level, 10, 67
  reliabilities, 64
  validity, 63
Ellis, A., 20, 27
Factor analysis, general
  biopolar factors, 5, 104–105

cluster analysis, 55
common factor process, 5
of *CPI*, 97
of *GZTS*, 103–104
of interest measurement, 47
of *MMPI*, 86
of personality measurement, 76, 78, 81
positive and negative correlations, 5, 31
Forbes, F. W., and Cottle, W. C., 8ff.
Fredericksen, N., 33
Fryer, D., 21, 31, 45
Gordon Personal Inventory, 80
Gordon Personal Profile, 80
Gough, H. G.
　MMPI, 6, 27, 82, 88, 95
　CPI, 96–103
Gough, H. G., *et al.*
　Dominance scale, 82, 95
　Responsibility scale, 82, 95
Gowan, J. C., 97
Guilford, J. P., and Zimmerman, W. S., 105
Guilford Zimmerman Temperament Survey
　construction, 103–105
　factor analysis, 103–104
　general, 79
　Guilford-Martin inventories, 104, 105
　high and low scores, 105
　intercorrelations, 105
　interpretation, 105
　omitted items, 104–105
　reliabilities, 105
　scales, 104
　scores, 105
　scoring and profiling, 104–105
　validities, 105
Guthrie, G. M., 89
Hahn, M. E., and MacLean, M. S., 46–47
Hanvik, L. J., 82, 95
Harris, R. E., and Lingoes, J. C., 93
Hathaway, S. R., 84
　and Briggs, P. F., 82, 94
　and McKinley, J. C., 6, 14, 76, 82, 85, 95
　and Meehl, P. E., 84, 89
Heilbrun, A., 100
Heston Personality Inventory, 79
Hicks, R. A., 97
Holland, J., 2, 48–49
Holzberg, J. D., and Alessi, S., 85
Horney, K., 3

Humm Wadsworth Temperament Scale, 3, 78
Inventories, general
　administration, 7, 20
　answer sheets, 7
　construction, 4, 31 ff, 50 ff
　content validity, 4
　correlations, 40–41, 76–78
　criterion groups, 4–6, 20, 50–53, 55, 59
　faking, 27–28
　instructions, 7
　interpretation, 4–5, 15, 21, 31 ff, 50 ff
　invasion of privacy, 23–27
　professional approach, 23, 29
　purpose, 19–21
　reliability, 13–14, 57, 72
　scoring, 12–13
　scoring service, 7, 12
　use of, 1–3, 7, 20–22, 29, 71
　validity, 14–15, 72–76
Item analysis
　and criterion groups, 5
　Kuder, 4, 5, 45
　of *GZTS*, 105
Items, general
　forced choice, 4, 31
　personality inventories, 70–71
　response-set, 4, 6, 33, 63
　validities, 72–73
　weighting, 4
Jackson, D. N., 97
Jackson, J. M., 105
Kleinmuntz, B., 3
Koponen, A., 64
Kuder, G. F., 6, 31, 32, 45–46, 48, 56–60
Kuder Preference Record-Personal, 79
Kuder Preference Record-Vocational
　construction, 56–58
　correlation with *MMPI*, 40
　correlation with *SVIB*, 41
　forms D and DD (*KOIS*), 57–58
　form E (*KGIS*), 59
　intercorrelation of scales, 41, 58
　interpretation, 58–60
　ipsative scores, 60
　reading level, 10, 58
　verification scores, 56–59
Kuder-Richardson Formula, 14
Kreidt, P. H., 6
Lebensohn, Z. M., 23, 25–27
Lee, E. A., and Thorpe, L. P., 46
Mallinson, C. G., and Crumrine, W. M., 60

Masculinity-femininity scales, 32–33, 37, 39, 84, 85, 91–92, 102, 105

Menninger, K., 19–20, 23

Minnesota Counseling Inventory, 80

Minnesota Multiphasic Personality Inventory
  anxiety index, 89
  character scales, 94
  coding system, 84
  construction, 82–86
  correlation with *Bell A.I.,* 77
  correlation with *KPRV,* 40
  correlation with *SVIB,* 40
  criterion groups, 84–85
  F minus K score, 28
  factor analysis, 86
  intercorrelation of scales, 76–77
  internalization ratio, 89
  interpretation, 87–95
  meaning of high scores, 87
  meaning of low scores, 87
  mood scales, 93
  most typical personality inventory, 80
  neurotic triad, 89
  N.C.S. new scales, 82, 94–95
  original clinical scales, 89
  patterns of scores, 87, 89, 90
  psychotic triad, 89
  reading level, 10, 86
  reliabilities, 85
  validating scales, 84, 87–89
  Welsh's factors, 89, 94

Minnesota Personality Scale, 5, 79–80

Minnesota Vocational Interest Inventory
  area scales, 61–62
  cluster analysis, 62
  construction, 60–61
  forms, 61
  interpretation, 61–63
  occupational scales, 61–62
  percentage of overlap, 61
  proposed use, 60
  shaded area, 62
  tradesmen-in-general, 60–61
  use with non-college bound, 62–63

Mitchell, J. V., Jr., and Pierce-Jones, J., 97

Mooney Problem Checklist, 79

Murray, H., 63

Myers Briggs Type Indicator, 79

National test scoring services
  Measurement Research Center, 12
  National Computer Systems, 12, 82–83, 94, 96

Testscor, 12

Navran, L., 82, 95

Nichols, R. C., and Schnell, R. R., 97

Norman, W. T., 61

Olheiser, Sister Mary David, 52

Perlman, M., 95

Personality inventories, general
  art of use, 3, 71
  computerized approach, 3
  contribution of, 3, 21
  correlations among, 76–78
  correlations with interest inventories, 41–42
  knowledge needed, 81
  problems of reliability, 72
  problems of validity, 72–77
  reading level, 9–11
  response set, 73–75
  structuring for use, 71
  use of, 34

Physician-in-general scale, 6

Psychologist-in-general scale, 6

Reading formulas, 8
  and grade level scores, 9, 11
  and selected standardized tests, 10
  and Thorndike word list, 9
  Dale-Chall, 8–9
  Flesch, 8–9
  Forbes and Cottle, 8 ff
  index of vocabulary difference, 11
  Lewerenz, 8–9
  Lorge, 8–9
  Yoakum, 8–9

Rosen, A., 86

Rothney, J., 52

Ruebhausen, O. M., and Brim, O. G., Jr., 27

Schmidt, H. O., 89

School Interest Inventory, 6

Schwebel, M., 52

Science Research Associates Youth Inventory, 79

Scores
  as interaction of individual and inventory, 32, 70
  correlation with ability, 38
  cumulative import, 21–22
  describing, 16–17, 32
  distortion of, 22, 27–28
  high and low, 31, 33–38, 53–54, 59, 87, 105
  ipsative, 17, 60, 67, 69, 70
  normal distribution, 53–54
  of average group, 16
  of noncollege groups, 38–39
  of norm groups, 16

reflecting relation among scales, 39
patterns, 53–56, 59
response set, 33–37, 53, 73–74, 97
standard, 53
strong emotion as bias, 37
use of, 3, 16–17, 21, 28
variable errors, 29, 55
Simon, W., and Hales, W. M., 90
Sims Score Card, 95
*Sixteen Personality Factor Question-
naire,* 79
Smith, K., 23
Social desirability response set, 6–7
Springob, H. K., and Struening, E. L.,
97
Strong, E. K., Jr., 20, 31, 32, 45, 46, 48,
51–56
and Tucker, A. C., 6, 52
Strong Vocational Interest Blanks
construction, 51–53
correlation with *KPRV,* 41
correlation with *MMPI,* 40
intercorrelation of scales, 41
interpretation, 53–56
managerial pattern, 55
reading level, 10
relationships within an occupational
group, 55
T 399, 51, 52
Super, D. E., 46, 78
and Crites, J. O., 31, 47, 48, 69,
78
Taylor Manifest Anxiety Scale, 88
Terman, L. M., 46
and Miles., C. C., 17
Thurstone, L. L., 31
Thurstone Temperament Schedule, 79–
80

Thorndike Junior Century Dictionary,
11
Tilton's percentage of overlap, 61
Trait-factor approach, 4
Tutton, Marie E., 60
Tyler, Leona E., 48
Vocational interests, general
acceptance-rejection theory, 31
center for research, 45
concepts, 30
contribution of, 3, 21
correlations among, 40, 41–44
correlation with personality inventories, 41–42
crystallization, 2, 32
direction of, 48
historical development, 45
information as evidence of, 30
manifest interests, 30
motivational aspects, 3
patterns, 50
point of reference, 5, 52–53
reading level, 9–11
statements about, 30
summary of theories, 46–49
types, 49
Weingarten's Picture Interest Inventory,
47
Welsh, G. S., 72, 76, 82, 84, 86, 89, 93,
94
Wheeler, W. M., *et al.,* 76, 86
Wiener, D., 100
Williams, H. L., 82, 95
Woodworth Psychoneurotic Inventory,
3
Yoakum, C. S., 45